Indie Author's Playbook

THE INDIE AUTHOR'S PLAYBOOK: ADVANCED STRATEGIES FOR THRIVING IN TODAY'S PUBLISHING WORLD

Multi-Award-Winning-Author
B Alan Bourgeois

B Alan Bourgeois

The Indie Author's Playbook: Advanced Strategies for Thriving in Today's Publishing World

© B Alan Bourgeois 2025

All rights reserved. No part of this publication may be reproduced, stored in a retrieval system, or transmitted in any form or by any means, electronic, mechanical, photocopying, recording, or otherwise, without the prior written permission of the publisher.

The information and opinions expressed in this book are believed to be accurate and reliable, but no responsibility or liability is assumed by the publisher for any errors, omissions, or any damages caused by the use of these products, procedures, or methods presented herein.

The book is sold and distributed on an "as is" basis without warranties of any kind, either expressed or implied, including but not limited to warranties of merchantability or fitness for a particular purpose. The purchaser or reader of this book assumes complete responsibility for the use of these materials and information.

Any legal disputes arising from the use of this book shall be governed by the laws of the jurisdiction where the book was purchased, without regard to its conflict of law provisions, and shall be resolved exclusively in the courts of that jurisdiction.

ISBN: 9798348462147

Publisher: Bourgeois Media & Consulting (BourgeoisMedia.com)

Indie Author's Playbook

B ALAN BOUERGEOIS

STORYTELLING
LITERACY & HERITAGE

Thank you for purchasing this limited edition book, offered in celebration of the author's 50-year milestone. Proceeds from your purchase support the Texas Authors Institute of History, a museum founded by the author in 2015, dedicated to preserving the legacy of Texas authors.

https://TexasAuthors.Institute

B Alan Bourgeois

Dear Fellow Authors,

I'm delighted to introduce this book—and every guide in this series—as a short, easy-to-read resource designed to help you succeed in your writing journey. As writers, our true passion lies in creating stories, and I understand that delving into the business side of publishing might not be where we wish to spend most of our time.

That's why I've made a conscious effort to keep things simple and straightforward, focusing on practical advice without unnecessary fluff. You'll find that some concepts overlap between books, and that's intentional—to reinforce key ideas and ensure that whichever guide you pick up, you're equipped with valuable tools to enhance your success.

I genuinely hope you find these guides enjoyable and helpful. Your feedback means the world to me, and I look forward to hearing about your experiences and triumphs.

Happy writing, and here's to your continued success!

Indie Author's Playbook

Introduction

Congratulations! By picking up this book, you've already taken a significant step toward mastering the next phase of your indie publishing career. Whether you've published one book or twenty, you've likely realized that sustained success as an indie author requires more than just talent and hard work—it demands strategy, innovation, and a deep understanding of the ever-changing publishing landscape.

This book is your guide to advanced strategies that go beyond the basics of writing, publishing, and marketing. While fundamentals like creating quality books and establishing a brand are essential, they're just the starting point. To thrive as an indie author in a competitive market, you need tools, techniques, and insights that will set you apart.

In these chapters, you'll discover:
- How to analyze your sales data to make smarter decisions.
- Creative ways to diversify your income through audiobooks, foreign rights, and merchandise.
- Advanced marketing techniques, from harnessing the power of BookTok to mastering multi-platform ad campaigns.
- The importance of cultivating long-term relationships with readers, fellow authors, and industry professionals.

Each chapter is packed with actionable advice, real-world examples, and case studies from successful indie authors. The goal is to give you a comprehensive understanding of what it takes to not just succeed, but thrive.

B Alan Bourgeois

You've already proven you have the passion and determination to self-publish. Now it's time to take your career to the next level. Let's dive in and unlock the strategies that will transform your writing dreams into a sustainable, flourishing business.

The chapters are outlined as follows:

1. **Understanding Your Audience at a Deeper Level**
   Discover advanced techniques for researching and connecting with your ideal readers.
2. **Leveraging Data to Drive Growth**
   Learn how to analyze sales reports, ad performance, and reader behavior to make data-driven decisions.
3. **Multi-Format Publishing Strategies**
   Maximize your reach and income by exploring audiobooks, hardbacks, and large print editions.
4. **Expanding into Global Markets**
   How to navigate foreign rights, translations, and international marketing to grow your audience worldwide.
5. **Crafting Evergreen Marketing Campaigns**
   Create marketing strategies that generate long-term results, from automated email funnels to seasonal promotions.
6. **Building and Engaging a Street Team**
   Assemble a group of passionate readers to help promote your books and amplify your marketing efforts.
7. **Advanced Advertising Techniques**
   Master multi-platform ad campaigns, retargeting strategies, and budget optimization for greater ROI.
8. **Collaborating with Influencers and Industry Partners**
   Build partnerships with BookTok creators, bloggers, and other authors to expand your reach.
9. **Branding Beyond the Page**
   Develop your personal brand to connect with readers across multiple touchpoints, from social media to speaking engagements.

10. **Exploring New Revenue Streams**
    Merchandise, courses, subscription services, and other ways to monetize your intellectual property.
11. **Managing Success and Scaling Your Career**
    Learn how to balance creativity with business as your career grows, including hiring support and managing your time effectively.
12. **Staying Ahead in a Dynamic Industry**
    Explore emerging trends in self-publishing, from AI-assisted writing tools to blockchain technology and NFTs.
13. **Sustaining Creativity for Long-Term Success**
    How to keep your passion alive while meeting the demands of a growing business.
14. **Refining Your Legacy**
    Build a body of work that stands the test of time and continues to earn for years to come.
15. **The Power of Community and Collaboration**
    Learn how to build relationships with fellow authors, readers, and industry professionals to create a supportive network.
16. **Your Advanced Author Blueprint**
    A comprehensive action plan for implementing the strategies in this book and tracking your progress toward success.

B Alan Bourgeois

Contents

1. Leveraging AI and Emerging Technologies — 9
2. Trends in Serialized Fiction — 13
3. Dealing with Piracy and Protecting Your Work — 18
4. Writing Your Author Business Plan — 23
5. Writing for Diverse and Global Audiences — 29
6. Building a Street Team or Fan Base — 34
7. Collaborating with Editors, Designers, and Other Professionals — 39
8. Sustainability and Environmental Impact of Self-Publishing — 45
9. Marketing for Introverted Authors — 50
10. Adaptability in Indie Publishing — 56
11. Celebrating Successes — 61
12. Ownership of Rights — 66
13. Innovative Marketing Strategies — 71
14. Community Support — 77
15. Sustainability and Longevity in an Indie Author Career — 83
16. The Indie Author Advantage — A Final Call to Action — 88

About the Author — 93
Other Books by the Author in this Series — 94

1
Leveraging AI and Emerging Technologies

Technology is changing the game for indie authors. From artificial intelligence (AI) writing tools to blockchain-based publishing, these advancements aren't just buzzwords—they're practical tools that can save time, boost creativity, and expand your reach. In this chapter, we'll explore how to integrate emerging technologies into your author career effectively.

AI for Writing and Editing
1. Idea Generation and Plotting
AI tools like ChatGPT, Jasper, or Sudowrite can help you brainstorm plot points, develop characters, or even refine dialogue. For example, if you're struggling with writer's block, tools like Sudowrite can suggest alternative ways to phrase a sentence or expand on an idea.

- **Use Case**: A fantasy author might use AI to develop unique magic systems by inputting parameters about their world. The AI generates possibilities the author can refine and integrate.

    Pro Tip: Treat AI as a collaborator, not a replacement. The best results come when you use its suggestions as starting points rather than final outputs.

2. Editing and Proofreading
AI-driven editing tools like Grammarly, Hemingway Editor, and ProWritingAid can streamline your revision process by catching grammatical errors, improving readability, and suggesting stylistic tweaks.

- **Example**: A romance author uses ProWritingAid to identify overused words and clichés, ensuring their prose feels fresh and polished.

Pro Tip: Pair AI tools with a professional editor. While AI can handle technical fixes, it lacks the nuanced understanding of tone and context that a human editor provides.

AI for Marketing
1. Automated Social Media Management
Tools like Hootsuite and Buffer use AI to analyze the best times to post, generate hashtag suggestions, and even craft content tailored to your audience.
- **Case Study**: A mystery author schedules a week's worth of Instagram posts using Buffer, leveraging AI insights to optimize posting times for maximum engagement.

2. Data Analysis for Ad Campaigns
Platforms like Facebook Ads Manager and Amazon Ads incorporate AI to analyze campaign performance. Use this data to tweak your audience targeting, ad copy, and budget allocation.
- **Example**: A science fiction author notices through Amazon Ads that their highest conversions come from targeting readers of Andy Weir. They adjust their budget to focus on this segment, doubling their return on investment (ROI).

Emerging Technologies in Publishing
1. Blockchain and NFTs
Blockchain technology offers secure, decentralized options for distributing and monetizing your books. Non-fungible tokens (NFTs) allow authors to sell limited-edition digital books or collectibles directly to fans.
- **Example**: An author creates 100 NFT editions of their latest novel, bundling each with exclusive bonus content

like deleted chapters or personalized messages. These editions sell out, generating buzz and additional income.

2. Augmented Reality (AR) and Interactive Books
AR technology can transform books into immersive experiences. Imagine readers scanning a page to see a 3D model of a fantasy map or hear a character's voice narrating a scene.
- **Example**: A children's book author partners with an AR developer to create interactive story elements that bring their illustrations to life, making their book a hit with tech-savvy parents and kids.

How to Get Started with AI and Tech

Step 1: Experiment with Free Tools
Start with free versions of tools like Grammarly or Jasper to get a feel for how they integrate into your workflow.

Step 2: Set Clear Goals
Decide where you need the most help—idea generation, editing, marketing—and focus your efforts there first.

Step 3: Stay Informed
Follow tech blogs, podcasts, or YouTube channels dedicated to writing and publishing tools to stay ahead of trends.

Recommended Resources:
- *The Creative Penn Podcast* by Joanna Penn (covers AI and blockchain).
- YouTube channels like *Self-Publishing with Dale* for practical tech tutorials.

Case Study: Joanna Penn's AI Revolution
Joanna Penn, a pioneer in indie publishing, has embraced AI to enhance her productivity. She uses tools like Sudowrite to brainstorm faster and ProWritingAid for precise editing.

B Alan Bourgeois

Additionally, she's explored blockchain publishing and NFTs to future-proof her career. Her willingness to adapt has allowed her to maintain relevance and lead discussions on the future of publishing.

Action Steps for Authors
1. **Choose One AI Tool**: Test it in your writing or marketing workflow. For example, use Grammarly for a chapter edit or Jasper for a blog post idea.
2. **Research Emerging Tech**: Learn about blockchain and NFTs to understand how they might fit your strategy.
3. **Embrace Change**: Allocate time each quarter to experiment with new tools or platforms that align with your goals.

Emerging technologies can seem overwhelming, but they're also empowering. By embracing AI and related tools, you can work smarter, not harder—freeing up time to focus on what matters most: your stories. In the next chapter, we'll explore another exciting frontier: serialized fiction and its growing appeal to readers.

2
Trends in Serialized Fiction

Serialized fiction is experiencing a renaissance. Platforms like Kindle Vella, Radish, and Wattpad have reignited interest in episodic storytelling, creating opportunities for indie authors to connect with readers in new ways. Writing in serialized format offers flexibility, reader engagement, and potential for continuous revenue, making it a valuable strategy for authors looking to diversify their offerings.

This chapter explores the rise of serialized fiction, how to structure episodic stories, and the platforms that can help you succeed.

The Rise of Serialized Fiction
Serialized storytelling isn't new. From Charles Dickens' *The Pickwick Papers* to Arthur Conan Doyle's Sherlock Holmes mysteries, many literary greats published their works in installments. The digital era has revived this format, with modern readers drawn to bite-sized episodes they can consume on-the-go.

Why Serialized Fiction is Popular
1. **Binge Culture**: Readers are accustomed to episodic content from TV series and streaming platforms, making serialized books an easy fit for their habits.
2. **Accessibility**: Shorter episodes are less intimidating and allow readers to sample stories before committing.
3. **Engagement**: Regularly released episodes create anticipation and build loyalty.

B Alan Bourgeois

> **Example**: A fantasy author on Kindle Vella releases a new episode every Wednesday, building excitement and encouraging readers to return weekly.

Advantages for Authors

1. Flexible Storytelling
Serialization lets you write and release content as you go, testing reader interest and adjusting your story based on feedback.
> **Pro Tip**: Use reader comments to refine future episodes or introduce new twists that align with what readers love.

2. Steady Revenue Streams
Many platforms allow authors to monetize individual episodes, earning consistent income over time.
- **Example**: On Radish, readers purchase "coins" to unlock episodes, giving authors a continuous flow of revenue.
-

3. Faster Publication
Instead of waiting until your manuscript is complete, you can start publishing episodes immediately, building an audience while you write.

Structuring Serialized Stories
Writing for serialization requires a different approach than traditional novels. Each episode must hook the reader, deliver a satisfying experience, and leave them eager for more.

1. Start with a Hook
The first episode is your chance to grab readers' attention. Introduce compelling characters and an intriguing premise right away.
> **Example**: In a thriller, the first episode might open with a murder witnessed by a seemingly innocent protagonist, setting the stage for the series.

2. Build Episodic Arcs
Each episode should have its own mini-arc, with a beginning, middle, and end. However, it should also contribute to the larger story.
> **Pro Tip**: Think of episodes as chapters that provide immediate gratification while advancing the overall plot.

3. End with a Cliffhanger
Cliffhangers keep readers coming back. Leave your audience with burning questions that make them eager for the next installment.
> **Example**: A romance author ends an episode with the protagonist catching their love interest in a compromising situation, leaving readers desperate to know the truth.

Top Platforms for Serialized Fiction

1. Kindle Vella
Best For: Authors with existing audiences on Amazon.
- **How It Works**: Readers purchase tokens to unlock episodes. Authors earn a share of the revenue.
- **Pro Tip**: Use Amazon's existing reach to cross-promote your serialized story with your published books.

2. Radish
Best For: Romance, fantasy, and mystery genres.
- **How It Works**: Radish targets mobile readers, with stories released in bite-sized chapters. Readers pay for early access to new episodes.
- **Pro Tip**: Focus on genres with high demand (e.g., steamy romance or suspenseful thrillers) to maximize engagement.

3. Wattpad
Best For: Building a loyal following through free content.

B Alan Bourgeois

- **How It Works**: Wattpad allows readers to interact directly with stories through comments. Authors can monetize through ads and premium content.
- **Pro Tip**: Engage actively with your readers on Wattpad to create a fanbase that will support future projects.

4. Royal Road
Best For: Fantasy and science fiction.

- **How It Works**: This platform is popular with niche genre readers. While monetization options are limited, it's a great way to build a dedicated audience.
- **Pro Tip**: Use Royal Road as a testing ground for new ideas before committing to full-length novels.

Marketing Serialized Fiction

1. Build Anticipation
Announce your episodes in advance and stick to a regular release schedule. Consistency is key to keeping readers engaged.

> **Example**: Use countdown posts on Instagram or Twitter to remind readers of upcoming episodes.

2. Offer Exclusive Perks
Encourage readers to support your work by offering early access or bonus content to subscribers.

> **Case Study**: An indie author on Radish rewards paying readers with behind-the-scenes notes on character development and alternate endings.

3. Cross-Promote
Leverage your existing platforms to direct readers to your serialized work. Mention it in newsletters, social media posts, and at the back of your published books.

> **Pro Tip**: Offer the first few episodes for free to hook readers, then monetize subsequent installments.

Case Study: Sarah Lin on Royal Road
Sarah Lin, a fantasy author, gained a massive following on Royal Road by releasing her serialized story *Street Cultivation* for free. The enthusiastic response led her to self-publish the full series on Amazon, where it became a bestseller. By building an audience through serialization, Lin turned a passion project into a thriving career.

Action Steps for Authors
1. **Choose Your Platform**: Research platforms that align with your genre and audience.
2. **Plan Your Release Schedule**: Decide how frequently you'll publish episodes to maintain momentum.
3. **Write Episodically**: Focus on hooks, arcs, and cliffhangers to keep readers engaged.
4. **Market Consistently**: Use social media and newsletters to build excitement and drive traffic to your serialized work.

Serialized fiction is more than a trend—it's a growing opportunity for indie authors to experiment, connect with readers, and generate steady income. In the next chapter, we'll address a crucial concern for all authors: protecting your work and combating piracy in the digital age.

3
Dealing with Piracy and Protecting Your Work

In the digital age, piracy is a reality that indie authors must contend with. While it can feel disheartening to see your hard work distributed without your permission, there are practical steps you can take to protect your intellectual property and minimize the impact of piracy on your career. This chapter explores strategies for preventing piracy, addressing it when it occurs, and turning your focus toward building a supportive, paying readership.

Understanding Digital Piracy

1. What Is Digital Piracy?
Digital piracy occurs when unauthorized copies of your work are distributed online without your consent. This often happens on torrent sites, file-sharing forums, or through unregulated e-book retailers.
> **Example**: A self-published romance author discovers their newly released novel available for free on a torrent site within days of publication.

2. The Impact on Indie Authors
Piracy can lead to financial losses and feelings of discouragement. However, it's essential to understand that not all downloads represent lost sales—many who pirate wouldn't have purchased the book in the first place.
> **Pro Tip**: Focus your energy on readers who value your work and are willing to pay for it, rather than obsessing over pirates.

Preventative Measures

1. Use Digital Rights Management (DRM)
DRM is a technology that restricts the copying and sharing of digital files. Many platforms, like Amazon KDP, allow you to enable DRM when uploading your e-books.
- **Pros**: Makes it harder for casual users to share your work illegally.
- **Cons**: Determined pirates can still bypass DRM protections.

Pro Tip: Weigh the potential deterrent effect of DRM against its limitations. It's not a foolproof solution but can discourage casual piracy.

2. Monitor for Unauthorized Copies
Regularly search for your book on piracy sites and forums. Tools like Google Alerts or specialized services like Blasty can notify you when your work appears online without authorization.
> **Action Step**: Set up Google Alerts for your book title and author name, so you're informed whenever they're mentioned online.

3. Watermark Your Files
For PDFs or direct e-book sales, consider embedding watermarks that include the buyer's name or email. This discourages unauthorized sharing.
- **Example**: A non-fiction author selling books through Gumroad uses personalized watermarks to remind readers that the file is intended for their personal use only.

4. Offer Free or Low-Cost Samples
Piracy often stems from readers wanting to "test" a book before committing to a purchase. By offering free previews, you can satisfy that curiosity while steering readers toward legitimate sales.

- **Example**: Provide the first 10–20% of your book as a free sample on your website or social media.

What to Do If Your Book Is Pirated

1. File a DMCA Takedown Request
The Digital Millennium Copyright Act (DMCA) allows you to request the removal of pirated content from websites. Most hosting providers and search engines comply with these requests.
- **How to File**: Identify the infringing site, locate its contact information (often listed under "DMCA" or "Copyright"), and send a takedown notice including proof of your copyright ownership.

   Pro Tip: Services like Blasty and DMCA.com can automate this process for a fee.

2. Focus on High-Impact Targets
Chasing down every pirated copy is exhausting and often not worth your time. Instead, focus on major piracy sources that might significantly affect your sales.

3. Redirect Traffic to Legitimate Channels
If you encounter pirated copies on forums or social media, post links to legitimate retailers alongside a message about how purchasing your book supports your ability to write more.
- **Example**: "I noticed some folks here sharing my book. Please consider buying it directly—it's only $3.99 on Amazon, and every sale helps me create more stories for you!"

Indie Author's Playbook

Building a Paying Readership

1. Cultivate Loyal Fans
Readers who connect with you personally are less likely to pirate your work. Focus on building a strong community through newsletters, social media, and personal interactions.
> **Example**: A sci-fi author offers exclusive short stories to newsletter subscribers, creating a sense of reciprocity that encourages readers to support their work legitimately.

2. Offer Added Value
Give readers incentives to purchase directly from you by bundling extras like bonus content, signed copies, or early access.
- **Example**: Sell e-books through your website with behind-the-scenes author notes or exclusive cover designs.

3. Educate Your Readers
Many readers don't realize the impact piracy has on authors. Use your platform to explain how their support makes it possible for you to continue writing.
- **Pro Tip**: Frame the message positively, focusing on gratitude for legitimate purchases rather than frustration with piracy.

> **Case Study: Lindsay Buroker's Balanced Approach**
> Fantasy author Lindsay Buroker has faced piracy, like many indie authors. Instead of letting it derail her efforts, she focuses on engaging her loyal fanbase and building trust with readers. By offering free samples and maintaining strong relationships with her audience, she ensures that her paying readers outweigh the pirates.

Action Steps for Authors
1. **Enable DRM**: Decide whether to apply DRM to your e-books when publishing.

2. **Set Up Alerts**: Use Google Alerts or a similar tool to monitor for unauthorized copies.
3. **File Takedown Notices**: When significant piracy occurs, act quickly to remove it.
4. **Build Your Community**: Focus on loyal readers who value and support your work.
5. **Educate Gently**: Help readers understand how their purchases support your career.

Piracy can be a frustrating reality, but by taking proactive steps and focusing on your paying readership, you can minimize its impact. In the next chapter, we'll shift gears to discuss building a professional foundation with a comprehensive author business plan.

4
Writing Your Author Business Plan

As an indie author, you're not just a writer—you're also an entrepreneur. Treating your author career as a business starts with a well-crafted plan. A comprehensive business plan gives you a roadmap to achieve your goals, maximize your revenue, and ensure your career is sustainable in the long run.

This chapter will guide you through creating a practical, actionable author business plan, with examples tailored to indie publishing.

Why You Need an Author Business Plan

1. Clarity and Focus
A business plan helps you define your goals and break them into actionable steps. Whether you're aiming to publish one book a year or build an expansive backlist, your plan provides direction.

2. Professionalism
Having a plan demonstrates that you take your career seriously. This mindset is essential when collaborating with editors, designers, or distributors.

3. Adaptability
A business plan isn't static—it evolves as you grow. Regularly revisiting and revising your plan keeps you aligned with your goals and helps you adapt to changes in the market.

B Alan Bourgeois

Key Components of an Author Business Plan
1. Your Vision and Mission
Your vision is your ultimate goal as an author, while your mission defines the purpose of your work. These guide every decision you make.

> **Example Vision Statement**:
> "To build a successful career as a fantasy author, publishing one new book every six months and growing a loyal global fanbase."
>
> **Example Mission Statement**:
> "To create immersive fantasy worlds that inspire readers to embrace adventure and imagination."

2. Market Research
Understanding your genre, audience, and competition is crucial. Research helps you position yourself effectively in the market.
Key Questions to Answer:
- What are the current trends in your genre?
- Who are your ideal readers, and what do they value?
- How do successful authors in your niche market their books?

Example: A romance author discovers that small-town contemporary romances with holiday themes are trending. They plan their next book series accordingly.

> **Pro Tip**: Use tools like Publisher Rocket or Google Trends to analyze keywords and market demand.

3. Financial Planning
A clear budget ensures you can manage your resources effectively and invest in the areas that matter most.
Budget Categories:
- Editing: $500–$2,000
- Cover Design: $300–$1,000

- Marketing: $200–$1,500 per book
- Software/Subscriptions: (e.g., Scrivener, Canva) $100–$300 annually

Example:
Monthly Budget:
- Advertising (Amazon and Facebook): $400
- Newsletter Growth Campaigns: $50

Revenue Projections:
- Goal: Sell 1,000 e-books at $4.99 each in Year 1
- Expected Royalties: $3,500 (after platform fees)

Pro Tip: Start small with marketing and increase your budget as your revenue grows. Track ROI (return on investment) to ensure your spending is effective.

4. Publishing Schedule

A publishing schedule helps you maintain consistency, which is key to building and retaining a readership.

Example Schedule:
- January–March: Write and edit Book 1
- April: Cover design, formatting, and pre-launch marketing
- May: Launch Book 1 and start writing Book 2
- November: Release Book 2

Pro Tip: Use tools like Notion, Trello, or Asana to organize your publishing timeline and track progress.

5. Marketing and Promotion

A robust marketing plan ensures your books reach the right audience.

Key Elements:
1. **Audience Building**: Focus on growing your newsletter, engaging on social media, and building a street team.
2. **Pre-Launch Campaigns**: Offer ARCs (Advanced Reader Copies) to generate early reviews and buzz.
3. **Advertising**: Experiment with Amazon Ads, BookBub, and Facebook Ads.

Example: A mystery author allocates $300 to Amazon Ads for their launch month, targeting readers of similar authors like Agatha Christie or Louise Penny.

6. Revenue Streams

Diversify your income to build financial resilience. Think beyond just e-books.

- Print books: Use platforms like IngramSpark or KDP Print.
- Audiobooks: Leverage ACX or Findaway Voices.
- Merchandise: Sell branded items like bookmarks or tote bags.
- Courses or Coaching: Teach writing or marketing to fellow authors.

Example: An indie thriller author earns 50% of their income from e-books, 30% from audiobooks, and 20% from speaking engagements.

Putting It All Together

Here's how a simplified business plan might look:

Author Business Plan Example

Vision:
To become a recognized name in sci-fi romance, publishing two books per year while building a fanbase of 10,000 readers.

Mission:
To tell stories that blend high-tech worlds with heartfelt love stories, inspiring readers to dream of possibilities.

Market Research:
- Genre Trend: Steamy sci-fi romances are trending, particularly with series.
- Ideal Reader: Women aged 25–45 who enjoy romance and sci-fi TV shows like *The Expanse*.

Budget:
- Editing: $1,000 per book
- Cover Design: $600 per book
- Advertising: $3,000 annually

Publishing Schedule:
- Book 1: Release in May
- Book 2: Release in November

Marketing Plan:
- Build newsletter to 1,000 subscribers through giveaways and lead magnets.
- Spend $500 on Amazon Ads per launch month.

Revenue Streams:
- E-books (70%)
- Print-on-demand (20%)
- Audiobooks (10%)

Tools and Resources for Your Plan
- **Google Sheets or Excel**: For budgeting and tracking expenses.
- **Trello or Asana**: For project management and scheduling.
- **Publisher Rocket**: For keyword research and market insights.
- **Wave or QuickBooks**: For tracking income and expenses.

Case Study: Mark Dawson's Business Savvy

Mark Dawson, an indie thriller author, used his business acumen to build a career generating six-figure income annually. He invests heavily in advertising, tracks ROI meticulously, and has diversified his revenue streams through e-books, audiobooks, and online courses. Dawson's approach highlights the importance of treating your author career like a business.

Action Steps for Authors

1. **Draft Your Vision and Mission**: Define your "why" as an author.
2. **Research Your Market**: Identify trends and understand your ideal readers.
3. **Create a Budget**: Outline expenses and revenue goals for your next book.

4. **Set a Schedule**: Plan your writing, editing, and publishing timeline.
5. **Develop a Marketing Plan**: Choose strategies to grow your audience and increase visibility.

By writing a detailed business plan, you take control of your author career and set yourself up for long-term success. In the next chapter, we'll dive into how to write for diverse and global audiences, ensuring your stories resonate across cultures and expand your readership worldwide.

5
Writing for Diverse and Global Audiences

The world of publishing is more connected than ever, and indie authors have the opportunity to reach readers across the globe. Writing for diverse and international audiences not only expands your potential readership but also enriches your stories by incorporating different perspectives and experiences. This chapter explores how to write authentically for diverse audiences, engage with global markets, and ensure your work resonates across cultures.

Why Diversity and Global Reach Matter

1. The Expanding Global Book Market
Digital platforms like Amazon, Kobo, and Google Play Books allow authors to sell in dozens of countries. Reaching international readers can significantly boost sales and open up new revenue streams.
- **Example**: Romance novels often sell well in English-speaking countries like Canada, Australia, and the UK, but emerging markets in India and Brazil are rapidly growing for e-books.

2. Reflecting Reality
Readers increasingly expect stories that reflect the diversity of the real world, whether through characters, settings, or themes. Writing inclusively can deepen your stories and broaden their appeal.

B Alan Bourgeois

How to Write Authentically for Diverse Audiences

1. Research Thoroughly
Authenticity begins with understanding. Research the cultural, historical, and social contexts of the people and places in your story.
- **Action Step**: If your book is set in Japan, immerse yourself in its culture by reading books by Japanese authors, watching films, and consulting reliable sources.

2. Avoid Stereotypes
Stereotypes reduce characters to clichés and can alienate readers. Focus on creating nuanced, multidimensional characters.
- **Example**: Instead of portraying a Latina character as solely "fiery and passionate," explore her hobbies, goals, and unique personality traits.

3. Use Sensitivity Readers
Sensitivity readers can help identify blind spots or inaccuracies in your portrayal of cultures, identities, or experiences.
- **Example**: If you're writing about a character with a disability, a sensitivity reader with that lived experience can provide invaluable feedback.

4. Incorporate Universal Themes
While cultural details add richness, universal themes like love, loss, or ambition resonate across borders. Ground your story in emotions and ideas that connect with readers worldwide.

Tips for Reaching Global Markets

1. Translate Your Work
Translations can significantly expand your readership. Start with languages in high-demand markets, such as Spanish, German, or French.

- **Platforms to Explore**: Use Babelcube or Reedsy to find professional translators.
- **Pro Tip**: Begin with your best-selling book to test the waters before investing in translations for your entire backlist.

2. Localize Marketing Efforts
Marketing strategies that work in one region may not resonate in another. Tailor your campaigns to local audiences.
- **Example**: In Germany, many readers prefer physical books over e-books, so consider leveraging print-on-demand services like IngramSpark to reach this market.

3. Understand Pricing Strategies
Adjust your pricing to reflect regional economic conditions. Lowering your prices in markets like India or Southeast Asia can make your books more accessible while increasing volume sales.
- **Action Step**: Use Amazon's regional pricing tool to optimize your prices for each market.

4. Leverage International Distribution
Distribute your books through platforms that have a strong presence in specific regions:
- **Kobo**: Popular in Canada and parts of Europe.
- **Google Play Books**: Gaining traction in Asia and Latin America.
- **Tolino**: A major player in German-speaking countries.

Case Studies: Writing for Global Audiences

1. Bella Andre's Global Success
Bella Andre, a bestselling romance author, expanded her readership by translating her books into multiple languages, including German and Italian. She also localized her marketing by running promotions specific to these regions. This strategy resulted in a significant boost in her international sales.

2. Mark Dawson's International Strategy
Mark Dawson uses targeted ads to reach readers in countries like the UK, Australia, and Canada. By tailoring his campaigns to reflect regional preferences, he maximized his reach while maintaining profitability.

Action Steps for Authors
1. **Research Your Target Market**: Identify regions where your genre is popular and learn about reader preferences.
2. **Invest in Authenticity**: Use sensitivity readers and conduct thorough research to ensure accurate representation.
3. **Experiment with Translations**: Translate one of your best-performing books and monitor its success before scaling up.
4. **Test Regional Marketing**: Tailor your campaigns and pricing to specific markets to optimize results.

Example: A Cozy Mystery Series Goes Global
An indie author writes a cozy mystery series set in a picturesque English village. After gaining a solid readership in the US, they decide to expand globally:
1. They hire a translator for German, knowing cozy mysteries are popular in Germany.
2. They release the German version with a culturally adapted cover that appeals to local tastes.
3. They run Amazon Ads targeting German readers who enjoy Agatha Christie and similar authors.
4. Within months, the German edition becomes a regional bestseller, doubling the series' overall revenue.

Writing for Diverse and Global Audiences: A Win-Win
By embracing diversity and reaching global markets, you not only increase your earning potential but also enrich your storytelling. Representation matters, and readers appreciate

authentic, well-crafted stories that reflect the breadth of human experience.

In the next chapter, we'll explore how to build and nurture a loyal street team or fan base—a vital component for sustaining your career and expanding your reach.

6
Building a Street Team or Fan Base

Your most loyal readers are your greatest advocates. A street team or fan base not only boosts your visibility but also helps spread the word about your books in authentic and impactful ways. Building and nurturing a community of superfans is a key strategy for indie authors looking to amplify their reach while strengthening reader relationships.

This chapter delves into how to create a dedicated fan base, recruit a street team, and empower them to become ambassadors for your work.

Why a Street Team Matters

A street team is a group of enthusiastic readers who actively support your books. These fans can play a critical role in your success by:
- Writing reviews and sharing your work on social media.
- Helping with book launches by spreading the word.
- Offering valuable feedback on early drafts or marketing ideas.

Case Study: Romance author Penny Reid uses her "Sharks of Awesome" street team to mobilize her fans for launches, giveaways, and promotions. This grassroots support has helped her consistently hit bestseller lists.

Steps to Build Your Street Team

1. Identify Your Ideal Team Members

Your street team should consist of readers who are genuinely passionate about your work. Look for fans who consistently engage with your content, leave reviews, or comment on your social media posts.

Pro Tip: Quality matters more than quantity. A small group of dedicated fans can be more effective than a large, disengaged one.

2. Create a Recruitment Strategy
Invite your most loyal readers to join your street team through personal outreach or open calls on your platforms.
> **Example**: Send an email to your newsletter subscribers with the subject line, "Want to Join My Inner Circle?" Include details about what being on your street team involves and the perks they'll receive.

3. Offer Incentives
Reward your street team members for their time and effort. Perks might include:
- Early access to your books (e.g., ARCs).
- Exclusive content like deleted scenes or bonus chapters.
- Personalized thank-you notes or signed copies.
- Swag like bookmarks, stickers, or tote bags.

Action Step: Use platforms like BookFunnel or StoryOrigin to distribute ARCs efficiently.

4. Set Clear Expectations
Communicate what you need from your street team. Common tasks include:
- Posting honest reviews on platforms like Amazon, Goodreads, and BookBub.
- Sharing promotional materials (e.g., book trailers, cover reveals) on social media.
- Participating in launch events, giveaways, or blog tours.

Pro Tip: Frame these requests as opportunities for them to help shape the success of your book, rather than obligations.

B Alan Bourgeois

Engaging Your Street Team

1. Build a Community
Create a dedicated space for your street team to connect, such as a private Facebook group, Discord server, or email chain.
> **Example**: Use a Facebook group to share updates, host discussions, and run fun challenges like "Guess the next book title" or "Vote on a cover design."

2. Show Gratitude
Recognize and appreciate your street team's efforts. Public shout-outs, exclusive perks, or even small personalized gifts can go a long way in fostering loyalty.
> **Example**: An indie thriller author sends personalized thank-you messages to their street team after a successful launch, emphasizing how their support made a difference.

3. Involve Them in the Process
Give your street team a sense of ownership by including them in key decisions.
- Let them vote on potential book covers or titles.
- Share sneak peeks of works in progress and ask for feedback.

Pro Tip: Poll your street team for ideas on how to market your next book—they might have creative suggestions you hadn't considered.

Growing Your Fan Base
A street team is part of a larger fan base that supports your career. Growing and nurturing this broader audience ensures a steady flow of new readers.

1. Build Your Newsletter List
Your email newsletter is the foundation of your fan base. Offer a freebie, like a short story or a novella, to encourage sign-ups.

Example: A fantasy author creates a free prequel to their series and offers it as a newsletter incentive, growing their list by thousands in just a few months.

2. Engage on Social Media

Consistent, meaningful interaction on platforms like Instagram, Twitter, or TikTok can help grow your audience.
- Post behind-the-scenes content, writing tips, or character profiles.
- Use hashtags relevant to your genre to reach new readers.

Pro Tip: Share user-generated content, such as fan art or reviews, to foster a sense of community and appreciation.

3. Host Reader Events

Virtual events, such as live Q&A sessions, cover reveals, or book launch parties, create excitement and strengthen connections.
- Platforms to Use: Facebook Live, Zoom, or YouTube.

Example: A sci-fi author hosts a virtual trivia night based on their book series, with prizes for the winners, generating buzz for their upcoming release.

Turning Fans into Advocates

Loyal fans are your best marketers because their enthusiasm is authentic. Empower them to spread the word:
- Provide shareable content like quote graphics or book trailers.
- Encourage them to tag you in social media posts.
- Run referral programs with rewards for readers who bring in new fans.

Case Study: J.F. Penn, an indie thriller author, gives her newsletter subscribers pre-designed social media graphics during her launches, making it easy for them to promote her books.

B Alan Bourgeois

Tools for Managing Your Street Team
- **BookFunnel**: Distribute ARCs securely to your team.
- **Canva**: Create promotional materials like social media graphics or bookmarks.
- **Google Forms**: Collect feedback or run polls.
- **Facebook Groups/Discord**: Build a private community for engagement and updates.

Case Study: Sarah J. Maas and Fan Loyalty
Though traditionally published, Sarah J. Maas serves as a masterclass in building a loyal fan base. Through regular interaction on social media, exclusive giveaways, and sharing her writing journey, she has cultivated a dedicated community. Her fans create art, cosplay as her characters, and eagerly promote her books on their own platforms—a blueprint any indie author can adapt.

Action Steps for Authors
1. **Recruit a Street Team**: Start with your most engaged readers and invite them to join your inner circle.
2. **Provide Value**: Offer exclusive perks like ARCs or behind-the-scenes content to make them feel special.
3. **Engage Consistently**: Build a community space and interact regularly to keep the team active and enthusiastic.
4. **Grow Your Fan Base**: Use newsletters, social media, and events to continually attract new readers.

A well-managed street team can be a game-changer for your indie author career. By fostering genuine relationships with your most passionate readers, you create a network of advocates who will champion your work far and wide.

In the next chapter, we'll explore how to collaborate effectively with editors, designers, and other professionals to elevate your books to the highest standards.

7
Collaborating with Editors, Designers, and Other Professionals

As an indie author, you wear many hats, but you don't have to do everything alone. Partnering with skilled professionals—editors, cover designers, formatters, and marketers—elevates the quality of your books and positions them to compete with traditionally published titles. This chapter explores how to find, vet, and collaborate effectively with the professionals who can help bring your creative vision to life.

Why Professional Collaborations Matter
Readers expect high-quality books, and delivering a polished product is essential for building trust and credibility. Investing in professional collaborators helps ensure your work meets or exceeds industry standards.

- **Example**: A professionally designed cover can increase a book's click-through rate on Amazon, directly impacting sales.

Pro Tip: View these collaborations as investments in your career, not just expenses. A strong product is more likely to yield long-term success.

Finding the Right Professionals

1. Editors
Types of Editing:
- **Developmental Editing**: Focuses on big-picture elements like plot structure, pacing, and character development.

- **Copyediting**: Polishes grammar, sentence structure, and consistency.
- **Proofreading**: Catches typos and formatting errors in the final draft.

Where to Find Editors:
- Reedsy: A curated marketplace of publishing professionals.
- Freelancer Platforms: Upwork, Fiverr, or Guru (check reviews and portfolios carefully).
- Referrals: Ask other authors for recommendations.

Example: A fantasy author hires a developmental editor to refine world-building and character arcs, ensuring their series has depth and coherence.

2. Cover Designers

Your cover is your book's first impression. A professional cover designer ensures your book looks compelling and marketable.

Qualities to Look For:
- Experience in your genre (e.g., romance covers differ greatly from thrillers).
- A portfolio showcasing a range of styles.

Where to Find Designers:
- 99designs: A platform where designers submit concepts based on your brief.
- Pre-made Cover Sites: Affordable, ready-to-use options (e.g., The Book Cover Designer).
- Independent Designers: Search on Instagram, Behance, or through author communities.

Pro Tip: Provide examples of covers you admire and clarify the mood and genre of your book during the briefing process.

3. Formatters

Formatting ensures your book looks professional across e-book and print formats. While tools like Vellum (for Mac users) and

Reedsy's free book editor make DIY formatting possible, hiring a professional formatter can save time and ensure precision.

Where to Find Formatters:
- Reedsy
- Fiverr (look for professionals with verified reviews).

4. Marketing and Publicity Experts
If you're launching a high-stakes project or trying to break into a new market, a marketing or publicity consultant can amplify your efforts.

Services Offered:
- Social media campaigns.
- Book blog tours and influencer outreach.
- Press release creation and distribution.

Example: A historical fiction author hires a marketer to coordinate a blog tour, generating reviews and visibility ahead of launch.

How to Vet Professionals
1. **Review Portfolios**: Look for work that aligns with your vision and genre.
2. **Check References**: Ask for testimonials from past clients or reviews on trusted platforms.
3. **Request a Trial or Sample**: Some editors and designers offer sample edits or mock-ups.
4. **Discuss Timelines**: Ensure their schedule aligns with your deadlines.

Red Flags:
- Poor communication or long delays in responses.
- A lack of portfolio or relevant experience.
- Overpromising results (e.g., "Guaranteed Amazon bestseller").

B Alan Bourgeois

Establishing Strong Working Relationships

1. Communicate Clearly
Provide detailed briefs or instructions to ensure everyone understands your expectations. For example:
- Editors: Share your target audience and genre expectations.
- Cover Designers: Provide genre-specific visual examples and key details like title, subtitle, and author name.

2. Set Boundaries and Agreements
Sign a contract or agreement that outlines:
- Deliverables (e.g., three rounds of edits, final cover file types).
- Payment terms (e.g., half upfront, half upon completion).
- Deadlines and timelines.

3. Respect Their Expertise
While it's important to share your vision, trust the professionals you hire. They bring experience and knowledge that can enhance your book.
> **Example**: A thriller author initially insists on a dark, minimalist cover but adjusts their vision after their designer explains why a bold, high-contrast cover aligns better with market trends.

Balancing DIY and Outsourcing
Not every task needs to be outsourced. Decide which areas you're comfortable handling and which require professional help.

DIY-Friendly Tasks:
- Social media content creation.
- Basic formatting (using Vellum or Scrivener).
- Writing newsletter updates.

Invest in Professionals For:
- Editing (essential for all authors).
- Cover design (critical for sales).

- Specialized marketing campaigns.

Budgeting for Professional Services
Set a realistic budget for your publishing expenses. Prioritize spending on elements that directly impact your book's quality and marketability.

- **Example Budget for a Romance Novel**:
  - Developmental Editing: $1,200
  - Cover Design: $500
  - Formatting: $150
  - Marketing: $400

Pro Tip: Reinvest royalties from your first book into professional services for your next release.

Case Study: Lindsay Buroker's Collaborative Success
Lindsay Buroker, a prolific indie fantasy author, emphasizes the importance of collaboration in her success. She regularly works with a team of editors, cover designers, and audiobook narrators to produce polished, professional products. By reinvesting her earnings into top-tier collaborators, she has built a brand that consistently draws readers.

Tools for Collaboration
- **Reedsy**: Hire editors, designers, and marketers.
- **Canva**: Create visuals for marketing campaigns.
- **Trello**: Organize and track collaboration tasks.
- **Dubsado**: Manage contracts and payments for professional services.

Action Steps for Authors
1. **Define Your Needs**: Identify which professional services will most benefit your next project.
2. **Research and Vet**: Spend time reviewing portfolios and gathering recommendations.

3. **Prepare a Brief**: Write a clear document outlining your expectations, timeline, and goals.
4. **Set a Budget**: Prioritize key investments like editing and cover design.
5. **Build Long-Term Relationships**: Cultivate trust and collaboration with professionals for future projects.

Collaborating with skilled professionals transforms your creative vision into a market-ready product. By finding the right team and maintaining strong relationships, you can ensure your books meet the highest standards and appeal to readers worldwide. In the next chapter, we'll discuss sustainability in indie publishing, exploring how to balance creativity, finances, and personal well-being for a lasting career.

8
Sustainability and Environmental Impact of Self-Publishing

The publishing industry is evolving alongside a growing global emphasis on sustainability. As an indie author, you have the power to make choices that align with eco-friendly practices while balancing financial and creative needs. This chapter explores the environmental impact of self-publishing and provides practical strategies to reduce your carbon footprint without compromising the quality or reach of your books.

Why Sustainability Matters in Self-Publishing

1. Reader Expectations Are Changing
Eco-conscious readers are increasingly drawn to brands and creators that prioritize sustainability. Showing that you care about the environment can strengthen your connection with these readers.
> **Example**: Highlighting your use of print-on-demand services (which minimize waste) in your marketing materials can resonate with eco-conscious audiences.

2. The Environmental Cost of Publishing
Traditional publishing generates significant waste from overprinting, unsold inventory, and paper production. Indie publishing, with its flexible print-on-demand (POD) model and digital-first strategies, inherently reduces waste but still has room for improvement.
- **Key Areas of Impact**: Paper usage, energy consumption from digital platforms, and shipping emissions.

B Alan Bourgeois

Eco-Friendly Practices for Indie Authors
1. Optimize Print Options
Print-on-demand (POD) services like Amazon KDP and IngramSpark eliminate the need for large print runs, reducing waste from unsold books.
- **Pro Tip**: Use POD for all print copies to avoid inventory surpluses.

Eco-Friendly Print Options:
- Choose smaller print sizes to reduce paper usage.
- Opt for cream-colored, recycled paper where available.

Example: A non-fiction author uses IngramSpark to offer eco-friendly editions printed on recycled paper, promoting this option in their marketing materials.

2. Prioritize Digital Formats
E-books and audiobooks are inherently sustainable, requiring no physical materials or shipping. By emphasizing these formats, you can lower your environmental footprint while reaching tech-savvy readers.
- **Action Step**: Launch your book as an e-book first, followed by a POD edition.

    Pro Tip: Offer exclusive bonuses (e.g., extra chapters or behind-the-scenes notes) for readers who choose digital formats.

3. Reduce Carbon Emissions in Distribution
Shipping physical books can contribute to carbon emissions, especially for international orders.
- **Solutions**:
  - Use POD services with local printing hubs to reduce shipping distances.
  - Encourage readers to buy from retailers that offer sustainable shipping practices.

> **Example**: An author suggests local readers order through Bookshop.org, which supports independent bookstores and reduces shipping impact.

Eco-Friendly Marketing

1. Minimize Physical Promotional Materials
Skip traditional printed bookmarks or flyers and focus on digital marketing assets like Instagram posts, email newsletters, and book trailers.

Eco-Friendly Swag Ideas:
- Reusable tote bags or bookmarks made from recycled materials.
- Plantable bookmarks embedded with seeds that grow into flowers or herbs.

> **Pro Tip**: Partner with sustainable vendors to create eco-conscious promotional items.

2. Host Virtual Events
Online book launches, Q&A sessions, and virtual signings eliminate the need for travel and printed materials. They're also cost-effective and accessible to global audiences.

> **Example**: A sci-fi author hosts a Zoom launch party, sharing behind-the-scenes stories about the book while inviting readers to ask questions live.

Managing Digital Sustainability
While digital formats reduce material waste, they still have an environmental impact due to energy use in data centers and devices.

1. Use Green Hosting Services
If you have an author website, choose hosting providers that run on renewable energy, like GreenGeeks or DreamHost.

2. Streamline File Sizes
Optimize your e-book and audiobook files to minimize data storage and transfer requirements. Tools like Calibre can help reduce file sizes without compromising quality.

Incorporating Sustainability into Your Brand
Making eco-conscious choices part of your author brand can enhance your appeal and inspire others to do the same.

1. Share Your Efforts
Be transparent about the steps you're taking to reduce your environmental impact. Highlight them in your marketing, on your website, and in interviews.
> **Example**: A mystery author includes a "sustainability statement" on their website, detailing their use of POD, digital-first releases, and partnerships with eco-friendly vendors.

2. Write Eco-Themed Stories
If it aligns with your genre, incorporate themes of sustainability and environmental awareness into your books.
> **Example**: A dystopian author sets their story in a future shaped by climate change, sparking conversations about sustainability among readers.

> ### Case Studies: Authors Embracing Sustainability
> ### 1. Joanna Penn's Green Publishing Journey
> Joanna Penn, an indie author and industry leader, actively shares her efforts to reduce her carbon footprint. She prioritizes e-books and audiobooks, uses POD for print, and partners with eco-conscious vendors. By being transparent about her choices, she has built trust and goodwill with her readers.

2. The Eco-Conscious Romance Author
A romance author launched a "green edition" of their book, printed on recycled paper with soy-based inks. They promoted the initiative through social media and attracted media attention, boosting both sales and awareness.

Action Steps for Authors
1. **Evaluate Your Current Practices**: Identify areas where you can make eco-friendly changes (e.g., switching to POD or prioritizing digital formats).
2. **Promote Your Efforts**: Highlight your sustainability initiatives in your marketing to appeal to eco-conscious readers.
3. **Partner Wisely**: Work with vendors and platforms that align with your values.
4. **Experiment with Green Swag**: Offer unique, sustainable promotional items that resonate with your audience.

The Bigger Picture
While no publishing process is entirely free of environmental impact, small, intentional changes can make a meaningful difference. By prioritizing sustainability, you not only reduce your footprint but also demonstrate your commitment to a greener future—a value that resonates with today's readers.

In the next chapter, we'll explore marketing for introverted authors, offering strategies to promote your work effectively without stepping too far out of your comfort zone.

9
Marketing for Introverted Authors

For many indie authors, the idea of marketing can feel overwhelming—especially for those who identify as introverts. Traditional marketing strategies often emphasize high-energy social interactions, public speaking, or constant self-promotion, which can be draining and intimidating. However, marketing doesn't have to push you out of your comfort zone to be effective.

This chapter explores strategies tailored for introverted authors to build an engaged audience and promote their work in ways that feel natural and sustainable.

Why Marketing Matters for Introverts
Marketing isn't about shouting the loudest or being the most visible; it's about creating meaningful connections with readers who value your work. Introverts are often skilled at deep, thoughtful interactions, which can be a powerful advantage in building loyal relationships.

Key Advantages for Introverts:
1. **Thoughtful Engagement**: Introverts tend to listen and respond deeply, creating strong reader bonds.
2. **Focus on Authenticity**: Authenticity resonates with readers, and introverts often excel at honest, meaningful communication.
3. **Preference for Quality Over Quantity**: A smaller, highly engaged audience can be more effective than a large, disconnected one.

Indie Author's Playbook

Strategies for Introverted Marketing

1. Leverage Asynchronous Communication
Engage with your audience on your own terms by focusing on platforms and methods that don't require immediate interaction.
Examples:
- Write blog posts or newsletters where you can share your thoughts at your own pace.
- Pre-schedule social media posts using tools like Buffer or Hootsuite to maintain consistency without daily engagement.

Case Study: A fantasy author who finds social media overwhelming focuses on writing a bi-weekly newsletter, sharing behind-the-scenes stories and book recommendations. This approach helps them connect with readers without draining their energy.

2. Build an Email Newsletter
Email marketing is one of the most effective tools for introverted authors. It allows you to communicate directly with readers in a controlled, thoughtful way.

Steps to Build Your Newsletter:
1. Offer an incentive for sign-ups, such as a free short story or bonus chapter.
2. Share content that adds value, like writing insights, updates on your books, or personal reflections.
3. Include calls-to-action (CTAs) that encourage readers to leave reviews or share your work.

Example: A mystery author grows their mailing list by offering a free prequel novella to subscribers, which not only attracts new readers but also builds excitement for their main series.

3. Emphasize One-on-One Interactions
Introverts often thrive in small, meaningful interactions. Focus on platforms where you can engage with readers personally without large audiences.
Options:
- Respond to comments or messages on Instagram or Twitter.
- Engage with individual readers via email.

Pro Tip: Set boundaries to prevent burnout. For example, allocate 30 minutes daily to reader interactions and then step away.

4. Create Long-Form Content
Introverts often excel at in-depth exploration of ideas. Long-form content like blog posts, podcast interviews, or YouTube videos allows you to showcase your expertise and connect with readers.
Examples:
- Write blog posts about your writing process, world-building, or research for your books.
- Record podcasts discussing themes in your work or sharing advice for other authors.

Case Study: Joanna Penn, an introverted author, built her audience through her podcast *The Creative Penn*. By providing valuable advice in a conversational format, she attracted a loyal following without having to engage in frequent social media interactions.

Leveraging Low-Pressure Social Media
Social media can be an effective tool for introverted authors if approached thoughtfully.

1. Choose the Right Platform
Focus on platforms that align with your strengths. For example:

- Instagram: Share visuals, like book covers or quotes, with minimal text.
- Pinterest: Create themed boards (e.g., character inspiration, book aesthetics).
- Twitter: Engage in short, focused conversations.

2. Batch and Schedule Content

Create a week or month's worth of posts in one sitting to minimize daily engagement. Tools like Later or Buffer can schedule posts for you.

3. Focus on Storytelling

Share snippets of your journey, behind-the-scenes moments, or insights into your characters. These posts feel more natural and less promotional.

> **Example**: A romance author posts a photo of their writing desk with the caption: "I spent all morning working on a big turning point for my heroine. She's about to take a leap of faith, and I hope readers will root for her!"

Introvert-Friendly Launch Strategies

1. Virtual Launch Events

Host a live event on platforms like Zoom or Facebook Live. Keep it low-key by preparing a brief presentation or Q&A session.

> **Example**: An introverted thriller author hosts a virtual book signing, where readers submit questions in advance. The author answers them live while signing personalized bookplates that will be mailed to attendees.

2. Partner with Influencers

Work with book bloggers, reviewers, and social media influencers who can promote your book to their audiences. This reduces the need for direct interaction while still generating buzz.

Pro Tip: Use platforms like NetGalley or StoryOrigin to connect with reviewers easily.

3. Utilize Paid Ads
Introverts can avoid constant self-promotion by using ads to reach readers. Platforms like Amazon Ads and Facebook Ads let you target specific demographics and genres, allowing the ads to work while you focus on other tasks.

Tools and Resources for Introverted Marketing
- **BookFunnel**: Share ARCs and exclusive content without direct engagement.
- **StoryOrigin**: Connect with reviewers and cross-promote with other authors.
- **Canva**: Design social media graphics or newsletter headers quickly and easily.
- **Hootsuite or Buffer**: Schedule social media posts in advance.

Case Study: Quiet Success with Emily St. John Mandel
Emily St. John Mandel, author of *Station Eleven*, is a self-described introvert. Instead of relying on constant social media activity, she focuses on long-form writing and occasional interviews to promote her work. Her thoughtful approach has earned her both critical acclaim and a devoted readership.

Action Steps for Introverted Authors
1. **Identify Low-Pressure Strategies**: Choose marketing methods that align with your strengths, such as newsletters or blog posts.
2. **Batch Your Efforts**: Dedicate focused time to create content in advance, minimizing daily stress.
3. **Set Boundaries**: Define how and when you'll interact with readers to avoid burnout.

4. **Leverage Tools**: Use scheduling platforms, email marketing tools, and paid ads to reduce direct engagement.
5. **Track Your Progress**: Regularly assess what's working and adjust your efforts to maximize impact.

Marketing doesn't have to feel overwhelming or exhausting. By focusing on strategies that play to your strengths, you can connect with readers in a meaningful way while maintaining your energy and creativity.

In the next chapter, we'll discuss how adaptability helps indie authors thrive in an ever-changing publishing landscape, preparing you to tackle new trends and challenges with confidence.

10
Adaptability in Indie Publishing

The publishing world is constantly evolving, with new trends, technologies, and platforms emerging every year. Successful indie authors thrive by embracing change and staying adaptable. Whether it's responding to shifts in reader preferences or exploring new distribution opportunities, adaptability is the key to sustaining a long-term career.

This chapter explores why adaptability matters, identifies areas where indie authors should remain flexible, and provides actionable strategies for navigating change with confidence.

The Importance of Adaptability

1. Staying Relevant in a Changing Market
Reader preferences evolve. Genres rise and fall in popularity, marketing strategies become outdated, and platforms adjust their algorithms. By staying flexible, you can pivot when necessary to meet new demands.
- **Example**: Cozy mysteries have enjoyed a resurgence in recent years, with readers seeking comforting, low-stakes stories. Authors who noticed this trend and pivoted to write in the genre tapped into a growing audience.

2. Leveraging New Technologies
Technological advancements, from AI tools to augmented reality (AR), create opportunities for indie authors to innovate. Authors who embrace these tools can streamline workflows, enhance their storytelling, and reach more readers.
- **Example**: A fantasy author uses AI software to create a 3D map of their fictional world, which they share with readers as an exclusive bonus.

3. Resilience During Industry Shifts
Platforms like Amazon KDP or Facebook Ads regularly update their policies or algorithms. Adaptable authors view these changes as opportunities rather than setbacks.
- **Pro Tip**: If your advertising performance dips after a platform update, test new targeting strategies instead of scaling back entirely.

Areas Where Indie Authors Must Stay Flexible

1. Writing and Publishing Schedules
While consistency is important, life events or market demands may require adjustments to your plans.
- **Example**: A romance author delays a book release to add a trending trope, such as the "grumpy/sunshine" dynamic, ensuring the book aligns with current reader preferences.

2. Genre Exploration
Readers' tastes shift, and some genres experience periodic surges in popularity. Experimenting with adjacent genres or blending elements from different genres can keep your writing fresh.
- **Case Study**: Lindsay Buroker transitioned from high fantasy to space opera, capturing a new audience while maintaining her signature style.

3. Marketing Strategies
What worked a year ago might not work today. Adapt your marketing approach based on platform trends, algorithm changes, and reader behavior.
- **Example**: Authors who embraced TikTok early leveraged its organic reach to sell thousands of books. Late adopters may need to focus on targeted ads or niche hashtags to find similar success.

4. Distribution Channels
Don't rely solely on one platform for your sales. Explore multiple distribution options to diversify your income.
- **Example**: Use Amazon KDP for e-books, IngramSpark for wide print distribution, and Findaway Voices for audiobooks.

Strategies for Embracing Adaptability

1. Stay Informed
Regularly read industry blogs, listen to podcasts, and participate in author forums to stay updated on trends and changes.
- **Recommended Resources**:
  - *The Creative Penn Podcast*
  - *The Self-Publishing Show*
  - Blogs by Reedsy, BookBub, and Jane Friedman

2. Experiment Regularly
Test new platforms, tools, and strategies to identify what works best for your career.
- **Example**: A thriller author tries serialized storytelling on Kindle Vella, learning valuable lessons about episodic pacing that they later apply to their full-length novels.

3. Track Metrics and Analyze Results
Use data to understand the impact of your efforts. Monitor book sales, ad performance, and reader engagement to identify areas for improvement.
- **Tools**: Amazon KDP Reports, BookReport, and Facebook Ads Manager.

4. Seek Reader Feedback
Your audience can provide invaluable insights about what they want. Use surveys, polls, or direct conversations to gather their input.

- **Example**: A non-fiction author asks newsletter subscribers which topics they'd like covered in future books, ensuring alignment with reader needs.

5. Collaborate with Other Authors
Networking with other indie authors helps you stay ahead of industry trends and discover effective strategies.
- **Action Step**: Join Facebook groups or attend virtual author conferences to exchange ideas and resources.

Case Studies in Adaptability
1. Hugh Howey's Serialized Success
Hugh Howey originally self-published *Wool* as a short story. Reader demand inspired him to expand it into a serialized novel, which became a bestseller and led to a traditional publishing deal. By listening to readers and adapting his approach, Howey built a thriving career.

2. Bella Andre's Transition to Wide Distribution
Bella Andre initially focused on Amazon KDP, but when competition increased, she expanded her reach by going wide with Kobo, Apple Books, and Google Play. This diversification strengthened her sales and insulated her from over-reliance on one platform.

Building a Long-Term Mindset
Adaptability is about more than reacting to immediate changes—it's about cultivating a mindset that embraces growth and learning.

1. View Setbacks as Opportunities
Every challenge is a chance to refine your approach. If a book launch underperforms, analyze the reasons and adjust your strategy for the next release.

2. Invest in Ongoing Education

Take courses, attend webinars, or read books on writing, marketing, and publishing. Staying educated helps you remain competitive.

Recommended Reads:
- *Let's Get Digital* by David Gaughran
- *Newsletter Ninja* by Tammi Labrecque

Action Steps for Authors
1. **Set Aside Experimentation Time**: Dedicate one day a month to testing new tools, platforms, or strategies.
2. **Monitor Trends**: Follow trusted industry sources to stay updated on changes and innovations.
3. **Diversify Your Efforts**: Expand your distribution, marketing channels, and genres to reduce risk.
4. **Gather Feedback**: Regularly ask readers what they want and adjust your plans accordingly.
5. **Stay Open to Change**: View adaptability as a strength, not a challenge, and embrace opportunities to grow.

Adaptability isn't about abandoning your goals—it's about finding new ways to achieve them. By staying flexible and proactive, you can navigate the dynamic world of indie publishing with confidence and resilience.

In the next chapter, we'll explore how to celebrate successes, both big and small, to stay motivated and maintain a positive mindset throughout your writing journey.

11
Celebrating Successes

As an indie author, it's easy to focus on what still needs to be done—reaching the next milestone, fixing the next problem, or chasing the next goal. However, recognizing and celebrating your achievements, no matter how small, is vital for maintaining motivation, boosting morale, and fueling your creativity. Celebrating successes helps you appreciate your progress, keep burnout at bay, and build momentum for future growth. This chapter explores why celebrating achievements is essential, how to recognize milestones, and practical ways to celebrate your wins—both big and small.

Why Celebrating Matters

1. Motivation and Momentum
Acknowledging your achievements reinforces the effort you've put into your career. Celebrating milestones keeps you energized and excited about the journey ahead.
- **Example**: Completing the first draft of a novel is a major accomplishment. Taking time to celebrate can motivate you to tackle revisions with renewed enthusiasm.

2. Building Confidence
Every win, no matter how small, is proof of your ability to succeed. Celebrating reminds you of your progress and helps build the confidence needed to tackle bigger challenges.
> **Pro Tip**: Keep a "win log" to track achievements like positive reviews, hitting word count goals, or learning a new skill. Revisiting this log during tough times can restore your confidence.

3. Reinforcing Habits
Celebrating milestones creates a positive feedback loop, encouraging you to keep pursuing your goals.
>**Example**: If you reward yourself after writing 1,000 words daily, the act of writing becomes associated with a sense of accomplishment and satisfaction.

Recognizing Milestones
Success isn't just about hitting bestseller lists or earning large royalties—it's about the steps you take along the way. Here are milestones worth celebrating:

1. Creative Milestones
- Finishing the first draft.
- Completing revisions or edits.
- Releasing a new book.

2. Marketing Achievements
- Growing your email list to a specific number.
- Successfully launching a book.
- Securing positive reviews from readers or influencers.

3. Personal Goals
- Overcoming writer's block.
- Learning a new skill, like running ads or formatting books.
- Establishing a sustainable writing routine.

How to Celebrate Success

1. Share Your Wins
Celebrate publicly with your readers, fellow authors, or support network. Sharing achievements helps you connect with others and build goodwill.
Examples:
- Post about completing your manuscript on social media.
- Thank your newsletter subscribers after a successful book launch.

2. Treat Yourself
Reward yourself with something meaningful when you hit a milestone. The reward doesn't have to be extravagant—what matters is that it feels special to you.
- **Ideas**:
    - A favorite meal or treat.
    - A new book or writing tool.
    - A short getaway or spa day.

3. Reflect on Your Journey
Take time to look back on how far you've come. Write in a journal, create a scrapbook of your milestones, or record a video reflecting on your achievements.
> **Pro Tip**: Reviewing your past successes can provide valuable perspective during periods of self-doubt.

4. Celebrate with Others
Involve your family, friends, or fellow authors in your celebrations. A launch party (virtual or in-person), dinner with friends, or a shared toast can make your achievements feel even more rewarding.
> **Example**: Host a virtual book launch where readers can join in the celebration. Include giveaways, live readings, and behind-the-scenes stories about your book.

Overcoming the Fear of Celebrating
Some authors hesitate to celebrate because they feel their achievements aren't "big enough" or worry about seeming boastful. However, every step forward is worth recognizing.

Reframe Your Thinking
- **Instead of**: "I only sold 100 copies this month."
- **Try**: "100 readers are enjoying my book—what an incredible start!"

B Alan Bourgeois

Pro Tip: Celebrating isn't about bragging; it's about honoring your hard work and inspiring others.

Incorporating Celebrations into Your Routine

1. Set Reward Triggers
Link specific achievements to rewards. For example:
- Completing your word count goal for the week = a favorite dessert.
- Releasing a book = a small vacation or shopping spree.
-

2. Schedule Reflection Time
At the end of each month or quarter, take time to reflect on what you've accomplished.
> **Action Step**: Write down three wins from the past month, no matter how small, and one way you plan to celebrate.

3. Create a Visual Representation of Success
Track your progress with tools like charts, vision boards, or milestone calendars. Seeing your progress visually reinforces how much you've achieved.
> **Example**: Use a whiteboard to track completed chapters or reviews earned, adding stickers or notes of encouragement as you go.

Case Studies: Authors Celebrating Successes

1. Colleen Hoover's Grassroots Celebration
Colleen Hoover, a bestselling romance author, credits much of her success to engaging with her readers. When her book *It Ends With Us* reached #1 on bestseller lists, she publicly thanked her fans through heartfelt social media posts and giveaways, making them feel part of her success.

2. Brandon Sanderson's Record-Breaking Kickstarter
When Brandon Sanderson launched his Kickstarter for surprise novels, he celebrated the project's overwhelming success with

regular updates, Q&A sessions, and fun reveals for his backers. His enthusiasm and gratitude deepened his connection with fans.

Action Steps for Authors
1. **Define Your Milestones**: List achievements you'd like to celebrate, from daily goals to long-term aspirations.
2. **Plan Rewards**: Decide how you'll celebrate each milestone, ensuring your rewards feel meaningful.
3. **Create a "Win Ritual"**: Develop a personal tradition for acknowledging successes, such as journaling or hosting a celebratory dinner.
4. **Share Your Wins**: Involve your readers and support network in your celebrations, building stronger connections.

Success isn't just about the destination—it's about every step of the journey. By celebrating your wins, you cultivate gratitude, joy, and a sense of accomplishment that fuels your ongoing growth as an author.

In the next chapter, we'll discuss ownership of rights and how indie authors can maximize creative and financial opportunities by retaining full control over their work.

12
Ownership of Rights

One of the greatest advantages of independent publishing is the ability to retain complete ownership of your intellectual property. Unlike traditionally published authors, indie authors maintain full control over how their work is used, distributed, and monetized. Ownership of rights empowers you to make decisions that align with your goals and ensures you benefit financially from your creativity in the long term.

This chapter explores the types of rights authors own, the benefits of retaining those rights, and how to maximize their value through licensing, partnerships, and strategic planning.

What Are Book Rights?
When you create a book, you own several rights associated with it. These rights govern how your work can be published, distributed, and adapted.

Types of Rights
1. **Print Rights**: The right to produce and sell physical copies of your book.
2. **Digital Rights**: The right to produce and distribute e-books.
3. **Audio Rights**: The right to produce audiobooks or other audio adaptations.
4. **Foreign Rights**: The right to translate and sell your book in other languages or countries.
5. **Film/TV Rights**: The right to adapt your book into movies, television shows, or other visual media.
6. **Merchandising Rights**: The right to create products (e.g., apparel, posters) based on your book.

Example: If you self-publish a fantasy novel, you own all these rights and can decide whether to retain or license them to others.

Benefits of Retaining Rights

1. Full Creative Control
Owning your rights means you have the final say in how your book is presented and adapted. You can approve or reject any proposed changes to your work.
- **Example**: A thriller author can ensure their cover design reflects the book's tone and aligns with their branding.

2. Financial Independence
When you own your rights, you retain all profits from your book. Traditional publishing often involves sharing royalties with publishers, agents, and other intermediaries, while indie authors keep the lion's share of their earnings.
- **Comparison**: A traditionally published author might earn 10–15% royalties on print sales, while an indie author using Amazon KDP typically earns 60–70% on e-books.

3. Long-Term Potential
Book rights can appreciate in value over time, especially as your readership grows. By retaining ownership, you can capitalize on future opportunities, such as foreign translations or film adaptations.
- **Case Study**: Hugh Howey retained the digital rights for *Wool* when licensing the print rights to a traditional publisher, ensuring he continued to profit from e-book sales while expanding his reach.

Maximizing the Value of Your Rights

1. Explore Licensing Opportunities
Licensing your rights allows you to collaborate with third parties while retaining ownership. For example:

- **Foreign Rights**: Work with a literary agent or rights manager to sell translation rights to publishers in other countries.
- **Audio Rights**: Partner with audiobook platforms like ACX or Findaway Voices to produce and distribute audiobooks.

Pro Tip: Negotiate limited licensing agreements, specifying the duration and scope of the deal, so you can reclaim rights later if needed.

2. Leverage Print, Digital, and Audio Formats

Publishing your book in multiple formats increases accessibility and revenue potential.

- **Example**: A romance author releases an e-book, print-on-demand paperback, and audiobook simultaneously, catering to different reader preferences.

3. Create Spin-Off Opportunities

Expand your intellectual property by creating related works, such as sequels, prequels, or short stories set in the same world.

- **Example**: An urban fantasy author writes a novella focusing on a fan-favorite side character, offering it as a bonus for newsletter subscribers or selling it as a standalone.

4. Adapt to Other Media

Explore opportunities to adapt your book into film, TV, or graphic novels. While these deals can be complex, they have the potential to significantly boost your book's visibility and revenue.

- **Action Step**: Partner with a literary agent who specializes in media adaptations to pitch your work to production companies.

Indie Author's Playbook

Protecting Your Rights

1. Register Your Copyright
In many countries, your work is automatically copyrighted when you create it, but registering the copyright adds an extra layer of protection.
- **How to Register**: In the US, visit the Copyright Office's website to file your application. Other countries have similar processes.

2. Use Contracts for Collaborations
Always use written contracts when licensing your rights or working with collaborators. Contracts should specify:
- The scope of the agreement (e.g., format, territory).
- Payment terms (e.g., royalties, advance payments).
- Duration of the deal.

Pro Tip: Hire an intellectual property attorney to review contracts and protect your interests.

3. Monitor Unauthorized Use
Stay vigilant for piracy or unauthorized adaptations of your work. Use tools like Google Alerts to track mentions of your book and take action when necessary (e.g., DMCA takedown notices).

Case Studies: Authors Retaining Control
1. J.K. Rowling's Merchandising Empire
By retaining merchandising rights for *Harry Potter*, J.K. Rowling built a billion-dollar franchise that includes toys, clothing, and theme parks.

2. Amanda Hocking's Strategic Licensing
Amanda Hocking self-published her paranormal romance novels and retained full rights, selling millions of copies. When she eventually signed a traditional publishing deal, she carefully negotiated terms to retain control over certain aspects of her work.

Action Steps for Authors
1. **Catalog Your Rights**: Create a list of all the rights associated with your books and note which ones are being used or licensed.
2. **Protect Your Work**: Register copyrights and use contracts to safeguard your intellectual property.
3. **Explore Licensing**: Identify opportunities to license rights for translations, audiobooks, or adaptations.
4. **Diversify Formats**: Publish your work in multiple formats to maximize revenue and reach.
5. **Consult Professionals**: Work with agents or attorneys when negotiating licensing deals to ensure fair terms.

Retaining ownership of your rights empowers you to shape your career, maximize your earnings, and explore new opportunities as your brand grows. By understanding the value of your intellectual property and protecting it effectively, you lay the foundation for long-term success.

In the next chapter, we'll dive into innovative marketing strategies that will help you stand out in a crowded market and capture the attention of new readers.

13
Innovative Marketing Strategies

Marketing can feel like an overwhelming task, but in today's competitive publishing landscape, it's a crucial part of an author's success. Indie authors have the unique advantage of being nimble, creative, and adaptable—qualities that allow for innovative approaches to reach readers.

This chapter explores cutting-edge marketing strategies to help you stand out in a crowded market, build a loyal audience, and boost your book sales. With a mix of proven tactics and fresh ideas, you'll find methods that align with your personality, resources, and goals.

Why Innovation Matters in Marketing

1. Readers Are Bombarded with Choices
With thousands of books published daily, readers are spoiled for choice. Innovative marketing helps your work grab their attention.
   Example: A suspense author uses a book trailer with interactive clues, engaging potential readers who enjoy solving mysteries.

2. Platforms Evolve Constantly
Social media algorithms and advertising trends change frequently. Staying ahead with creative strategies ensures your efforts remain effective.

3. Standing Out Builds Longevity

B Alan Bourgeois

Innovative marketing creates memorable experiences for readers, fostering loyalty and encouraging word-of-mouth promotion.

Innovative Strategies for Indie Authors

1. Create Unique Reader Experiences
Craft experiences that immerse your audience in your book's world.
- **Interactive Elements**: Add QR codes in your book that lead to exclusive maps, character art, or playlists.
- **Example**: A fantasy author includes a QR code at the end of their novel, leading readers to a downloadable short story set in their book's universe.

2. Leverage TikTok and Reels
Short-form video content is a powerful way to connect with readers. Platforms like TikTok and Instagram Reels are especially effective for book promotion.
- **Ideas for Posts**:
    - Share "aesthetic" videos of your book's mood or themes.
    - Record behind-the-scenes clips of your writing process.
    - Use trending sounds to create bookish content.
- **Case Study**: Romance author Emily Henry gained significant traction by using TikTok trends to showcase her books' themes, attracting a large, engaged audience.

3. Host Creative Virtual Events
Virtual events are an affordable, low-pressure way to engage readers worldwide.
- **Ideas**:
    - Virtual Book Club: Host discussions about your book and answer reader questions.
    - Writing Workshops: Offer a session on how you developed your world or characters.

- "Ask Me Anything" (AMA): Use platforms like Reddit or Instagram Stories for live Q&A sessions.

Pro Tip: Partner with fellow authors to co-host events and reach a broader audience.

4. Gamify Your Marketing
Turn your promotions into fun, interactive games to engage readers.

Example: A sci-fi author creates a "choose-your-own-adventure" marketing campaign on Instagram Stories, allowing followers to vote on plot twists related to their book.

5. Collaborate with Influencers
Partnering with book bloggers, Bookstagrammers, or BookTok creators can help you tap into an existing audience of avid readers.

Action Step: Use platforms like BookSirens or NetGalley to connect with reviewers and influencers.

Pro Tip: Offer influencers exclusive content, such as sneak peeks or behind-the-scenes insights, to incentivize promotion.

6. Experiment with Serialized Content
Platforms like Kindle Vella, Wattpad, or Radish allow you to publish your book in installments, keeping readers engaged over time. Serialized content can also act as a testing ground for new ideas.

Case Study: Author Bethany Atazadeh used serialized storytelling on Wattpad to build an audience before launching her self-published books, resulting in strong sales and loyal fans.

Innovative Advertising Approaches

1. Use Dynamic Targeting
Instead of targeting broad audiences, refine your ads to reach niche groups.

B Alan Bourgeois

> **Example**: A historical fiction author targets readers of popular historical novels like *The Nightingale* by using Amazon Ads' "Product Targeting" feature.

2. Retarget Website Visitors
Set up Facebook Pixel or Google Analytics on your author website to track visitors and serve them tailored ads later.
> **Pro Tip**: Offer a freebie, like a novella or resource guide, to collect email addresses for retargeting campaigns.

3. Offer Limited-Time Bundles
Collaborate with other authors in your genre to create discounted e-book bundles.
> **Example**: A group of cozy mystery authors bundles their first-in-series books into a $0.99 deal, promoting the bundle to each other's audiences.

Building Long-Term Strategies
1. Invest in Your Brand
Your brand is the sum of how readers perceive you. Develop consistent visuals, tone, and messaging across your website, social media, and books.
> **Example**: A thriller author uses dark, suspenseful imagery on their book covers, website, and Instagram posts, reinforcing their brand.

2. Build a Street Team
Recruit passionate readers to help promote your books. Your street team can write reviews, share social media posts, and spread the word about your work.
> **Pro Tip**: Reward your team with ARCs, exclusive content, or small gifts.

3. Focus on Community Engagement
Readers are more likely to support authors who make them feel valued. Build meaningful relationships through:

- Email newsletters that include personal updates or behind-the-scenes insights.
- Social media interactions that prioritize genuine conversation over self-promotion.

Case Studies: Innovative Marketing in Action

1. Neil Gaiman's Virtual Signings
Neil Gaiman offered virtual signings where readers submitted questions in advance. He answered them live while signing personalized bookplates, creating an intimate, memorable experience for fans.

2. Colleen Hoover's Social Media Engagement
Colleen Hoover engages readers by sharing humorous, heartfelt, and behind-the-scenes content on social media. Her relatable posts build strong connections, fueling word-of-mouth promotion.

Action Steps for Authors
1. **Experiment with One New Strategy**: Choose a fresh tactic, such as TikTok videos or an interactive virtual event, to test with your next release.
2. **Partner with Influencers**: Identify 5–10 Bookstagrammers or BookTok creators in your genre and reach out with collaboration ideas.
3. **Engage Your Audience**: Poll your readers about their preferences and tailor your marketing efforts accordingly.
4. **Analyze Results**: Use metrics to track the performance of innovative campaigns, refining your approach over time.

Innovative marketing is about thinking outside the box to create meaningful, memorable connections with readers. By experimenting with creative strategies, leveraging the latest platforms, and focusing on engagement, you can set your books apart in a crowded marketplace.

B Alan Bourgeois

In the next chapter, we'll explore the power of community support and how connecting with other authors and readers can elevate your career.

14
Community Support

The indie author journey can feel solitary at times, but building and leveraging a supportive community is one of the most effective ways to grow your career. Connecting with other authors, readers, and professionals not only provides valuable resources and insights but also creates a network that amplifies your reach and success.

This chapter explores the importance of community support, strategies for building relationships, and ways to give back to the indie author ecosystem while strengthening your own career.

The Value of Community in Indie Publishing

1. Emotional Support
Writing and publishing come with challenges, from creative roadblocks to disappointing sales. A supportive community offers encouragement and empathy to help you stay motivated.
   Example: An author struggling with writer's block shares their frustrations in a writing group, receiving advice and support that reignites their creativity.

2. Shared Knowledge
No one has all the answers, but within a community, you can learn from others' experiences, saving time and avoiding common pitfalls.
   Pro Tip: Join communities that align with your specific goals, such as marketing strategies, genre expertise, or craft development.

3. Cross-Promotion Opportunities
Collaborating with other authors expands your audience and boosts visibility.
   Example: A group of fantasy authors organizes a themed giveaway, pooling their audiences to promote their books collectively.

How to Build Your Author Community

1. Engage with Fellow Authors
Connect with other writers to share experiences, tips, and resources.
- **Where to Find Them**:
    - Writing forums like Absolute Write or Kboards.
    - Facebook groups tailored to indie authors (e.g., 20BooksTo50K).
    - In-person or virtual writing conferences, such as those hosted by Writer's Digest or Reedsy.

Pro Tip: Start by engaging authentically—comment on posts, share advice, or congratulate peers on their successes. Relationships grow organically through mutual support.

2. Collaborate on Projects
Joint ventures are a win-win for authors and readers.
   Examples:
- Anthologies: A romance author teams up with peers to create a holiday-themed short story collection, boosting exposure for all contributors.
- Co-Writing: Two authors with complementary styles co-write a novel, combining their audiences for a successful release.
- Shared Events: Host a virtual panel or discussion with other authors in your genre.

3. Connect with Readers
Your readers are an essential part of your community. Fostering genuine relationships with them builds loyalty and transforms casual readers into lifelong fans.
- **Strategies**:
    - Engage in reader groups on platforms like Facebook or Goodreads.
    - Respond to fan emails or social media comments with gratitude.
    - Host Q&A sessions, either live or through newsletters.

Example: An author creates a private Facebook group for fans, where they share updates, exclusive content, and fun challenges related to their books.

4. Network with Professionals
Editors, designers, marketers, and other publishing professionals can offer guidance and opportunities.
Action Step: Attend webinars or workshops led by industry experts to learn and make connections.
Pro Tip: Follow up with a personalized thank-you note or email to foster long-term relationships.

Giving Back to the Community
Supporting others in the indie publishing space strengthens the ecosystem and builds goodwill.

1. Share Your Knowledge
Pass along what you've learned to help newer authors.
Example: Write a blog post about your experience with running Amazon Ads, providing tips for others.

2. Offer Mentorship
If you're an experienced author, mentoring a newcomer can be incredibly rewarding.
Pro Tip: Set boundaries to ensure your guidance fits within your schedule and expertise.

3. Promote Fellow Authors
Celebrate others' successes and share their work with your audience.
- **Action Step**: Post about a peer's book release on social media or include it in your newsletter.

Example: A thriller author highlights a new book by a fellow writer in their genre, encouraging readers to check it out.

Leveraging Community for Growth
1. Cross-Promote Newsletters
Swap newsletter mentions with other authors in your genre to introduce your work to new readers.
Pro Tip: Choose authors with similar-sized audiences for mutual benefit.

2. Share Costs and Resources
Collaborating with others can lower expenses and streamline processes.
Example: A group of indie authors pools funds to hire a professional editor for an anthology.

3. Build Long-Term Relationships
Focus on creating genuine, lasting connections rather than transactional ones. These relationships often lead to unexpected opportunities.
Case Study: Two indie authors who meet at a conference later collaborate on a podcast, growing both their audiences.

Case Studies: Success Through Community

1. Lindsay Buroker's Author Network
Lindsay Buroker, a successful indie author, credits much of her success to her involvement in author communities. By participating in forums, sharing tips, and collaborating on promotions, she's built a loyal audience and a thriving career.

2. The Anthology Advantage

A group of sci-fi authors joined forces to create an anthology. By combining their marketing efforts and reaching each other's audiences, the anthology became a bestseller in its category, increasing visibility for all contributors.

Tools for Community Engagement

- **Facebook Groups**: Join or create groups for authors and readers in your niche.
- **Slack or Discord**: Use these platforms for private, focused discussions with collaborators or fans.
- **StoryOrigin and BookFunnel**: Tools for cross-promotion and newsletter swaps.
- **Zoom or StreamYard**: Host virtual events with ease.

Action Steps for Authors

1. **Join a New Community**: Research and participate in one online group or forum related to your genre or publishing goals.
2. **Collaborate with an Author**: Reach out to a peer to discuss joint promotions, anthologies, or other collaborative projects.
3. **Engage Your Readers**: Start a private group or newsletter segment dedicated to interacting with your fans.
4. **Support Others**: Promote a fellow author's work or share a helpful resource with your community.

The indie publishing journey is far more rewarding when you're part of a supportive community. By building relationships, collaborating with others, and giving back, you can create a network that enriches your career and fosters mutual success.

In the next chapter, we'll discuss how adaptability, creativity, and perseverance come together to shape a sustainable and fulfilling author career.

B Alan Bourgeois

15
Sustainability and Longevity in an Indie Author Career

The path to becoming a successful indie author isn't a sprint; it's a marathon. To achieve long-term success, you must balance creative fulfillment with financial stability, personal well-being, and adaptability to an ever-changing industry. Sustainability is about building a career that supports you—not just financially but emotionally and creatively—while creating a legacy that continues to grow over time.

In this chapter, we'll explore strategies for maintaining longevity as an indie author, including balancing work and life, managing finances, and nurturing your creativity.

The Pillars of a Sustainable Author Career

1. Consistency in Publishing

Frequent, high-quality releases keep readers engaged and help grow your audience. However, sustainability means balancing productivity with maintaining your well-being and ensuring the quality of your work.

Strategies:
- Create a realistic publishing schedule that aligns with your writing pace.
- Build a backlog of finished works before launching a series, allowing for consistent releases.

Example: A mystery author writes three books in a series before releasing the first, ensuring they can maintain a steady publication rhythm without feeling rushed.

2. Financial Planning and Stability
A sustainable career requires managing your income effectively and reinvesting in your business.
Key Tips:
- **Diversify Income Streams**: Beyond book sales, explore options like audiobooks, merchandise, speaking engagements, or teaching workshops.
- **Track Expenses and Revenue**: Use tools like QuickBooks or Excel to monitor your finances, ensuring you stay within budget.
- **Reinvest Wisely**: Allocate a portion of your royalties toward professional editing, cover design, or marketing to improve your product and expand your reach.

Pro Tip: Keep an emergency fund to cushion against fluctuations in book sales or unexpected expenses.

3. Work-Life Balance
Burnout is a significant risk for indie authors who juggle writing, marketing, and personal responsibilities. Prioritizing self-care and setting boundaries helps ensure longevity.
Practical Steps:
- Set specific work hours for writing and publishing tasks, leaving time for relaxation and family.
- Take regular breaks between projects to recharge your creativity.
- Delegate tasks when possible, such as hiring a virtual assistant to handle administrative duties.

Example: An author schedules "writing sprints" in the morning and reserves afternoons for non-writing activities like exercise or spending time with loved ones.

4. Evolving with the Industry
The publishing world is constantly changing. Staying open to new trends and technologies ensures your career remains relevant.
Action Steps:

- Attend webinars or conferences to learn about new platforms, tools, and marketing strategies.
- Experiment with emerging formats, like serialized fiction on platforms like Kindle Vella or Radish.
- Monitor reader preferences by engaging with your audience and studying market trends.

Case Study: A romance author adapts to the growing audiobook market by producing high-quality audio editions of their books, doubling their income and reaching new readers.

Nurturing Your Creativity
1. Protect Your Passion for Writing
The demands of indie publishing can sometimes overshadow the joy of storytelling. Reconnecting with your creative purpose keeps your passion alive.

Tips:
- Write for yourself occasionally, without worrying about market trends or deadlines.
- Experiment with new genres or formats to reignite your enthusiasm.
- Celebrate milestones, like completing a draft, to remind yourself of your progress.

2. Learn Continuously
Continual learning not only hones your craft but also keeps you inspired.
- Take writing courses or read books on storytelling and character development.
- Join critique groups or writing communities to exchange feedback and ideas.
- Study successful authors in your genre to identify techniques that resonate with readers.

3. Accept Creative Cycles
Not every period will be equally productive. Embrace the natural ebb and flow of creativity instead of forcing progress during slow periods.
> **Pro Tip**: Use downtime for research, outlining, or brainstorming new projects.

Legacy Building: Thinking Beyond the Present
1. Building a Backlist
A strong backlist is one of the most reliable ways to ensure long-term income. Older titles continue to generate revenue while attracting new readers to your current releases.
Strategy: Periodically update or rebrand older books with refreshed covers, updated formatting, or bonus content to keep them relevant.

2. Expanding Your Brand
Consider how your author brand can grow beyond books.
- Merchandise: Create branded products like mugs, tote bags, or bookmarks related to your books.
- Adaptations: Explore opportunities for your stories to be adapted into film, TV, or graphic novels.
- Teaching: Share your knowledge through courses, workshops, or consulting for aspiring authors.

3. Leaving a Creative Legacy
Your books are a lasting contribution to the literary world. Thinking long-term about your goals ensures that your career has a lasting impact.
> **Example**: An author creates a fantasy series with interconnected worlds, laying the foundation for spin-offs and companion stories that can be developed over years.

Case Studies: Long-Term Success Stories
1. Joanna Penn's Multifaceted Career
Joanna Penn balances writing fiction with sharing resources for other authors. By diversifying her income

through books, podcasts, courses, and public speaking, she has built a sustainable and fulfilling career.

2. Lindsay Buroker's Backlist Success
With dozens of titles in her catalog, Lindsay Buroker continues to earn from her older works while consistently releasing new ones. Her strategic reinvestment in marketing and audiobook production has kept her backlist thriving.

Action Steps for Authors
1. **Plan for the Long Term**: Set goals for the next 1, 3, and 5 years, focusing on both creative and financial milestones.
2. **Diversify Your Efforts**: Explore additional income streams and experiment with new formats or platforms.
3. **Prioritize Well-Being**: Schedule time for self-care and maintain boundaries to avoid burnout.
4. **Invest in Your Craft**: Commit to ongoing learning and creative exploration to keep your writing fresh.
5. **Review and Adapt**: Regularly assess your strategies, making adjustments based on market trends and personal growth.

Sustainability in indie publishing requires a balance of creativity, business acumen, and self-care. By planning thoughtfully, adapting to change, and nurturing your passion, you can build a career that not only supports you financially but also fulfills you personally.

In the next chapter, we'll conclude with an empowering overview of the indie author journey and actionable steps to take your career to the next level.

16
The Indie Author Advantage — A Final Call to Action

The world of indie publishing offers opportunities that traditional publishing simply cannot match. It empowers authors with creative freedom, financial control, and the ability to build direct connections with readers. Yet, succeeding as an indie author requires more than just talent—it takes strategic planning, adaptability, and persistence.

This chapter serves as both a reflection on the advantages of indie publishing and a call to action for authors ready to take control of their careers. It will summarize the lessons shared throughout this book and provide actionable steps to help you achieve your publishing goals.

Embracing the Indie Author Advantage
1. Mastering Control

As an indie author, you have full control over every aspect of your publishing journey—from the content of your books to their presentation and marketing. This is both a privilege and a responsibility.

- **Key Takeaway**: Your vision drives every decision. By learning the fundamentals of cover design, formatting, and branding, you ensure your books resonate with your target audience.
- **Action Step**: Write down three areas of the publishing process you'd like to improve (e.g., cover design, ad targeting, social media presence) and commit to learning or outsourcing those tasks.

Indie Author's Playbook

2. Maximizing Royalties
Indie publishing allows you to retain the majority of your earnings, unlike traditional publishing models. However, maximizing royalties means understanding pricing, distribution, and the platforms that best serve your goals.
- **Key Takeaway**: Diversifying your income streams—through wide distribution, audiobooks, and even merchandise—creates a more sustainable career.
- **Action Step**: Evaluate your current sales channels and explore opportunities to expand into new formats, such as print-on-demand or audiobooks.

3. Reaching Readers
Reaching readers requires more than just publishing your book; it demands consistent marketing and engagement. The indie author advantage lies in your ability to build direct, meaningful relationships with your audience.
- **Key Takeaway**: By understanding your readers' preferences and creating tailored marketing campaigns, you can foster loyalty and word-of-mouth promotion.
- **Action Step**: Identify your ideal reader (age, genre preference, interests) and craft a marketing plan that directly appeals to them, including newsletters, social media, or targeted ads.

The Path Forward: Your Next Steps

1. Set Clear Goals
Define what success means to you. Whether it's financial independence, creative fulfillment, or a specific sales milestone, having a clear goal will guide your decisions.
Exercise: Write down your 1-year, 3-year, and 5-year goals as an indie author. Break each goal into actionable steps.

2. Develop a Systematic Approach

The most successful indie authors treat their careers like a business. This means creating systems for writing, publishing, and marketing that are repeatable and scalable.

Example:
- **Writing System**: Commit to a daily or weekly word count goal.
- **Publishing System**: Create a checklist for each book's production (editing, cover design, formatting, launch).
- **Marketing System**: Use tools like scheduling platforms for social media and email newsletters to maintain consistent engagement.

3. Build a Support Network

Surround yourself with like-minded authors, industry professionals, and enthusiastic readers who can support and inspire you.

- **Action Step**: Join one new community or network this month, whether it's a Facebook group, a writing forum, or a local author meetup.

4. Embrace Continuous Learning

The indie publishing landscape is always changing. To stay competitive, commit to lifelong learning about new tools, platforms, and strategies.

> **Pro Tip**: Set aside time each quarter to read a book, take a course, or attend a webinar related to publishing or marketing.

5. Celebrate Your Wins

Every milestone matters. Taking time to acknowledge your progress, no matter how small, keeps you motivated and connected to your passion.

> **Exercise**: Reflect on three achievements from your indie publishing journey so far and plan a way to celebrate each one.

A Vision for the Future
Imagine this:
- Your books are reaching readers around the globe.
- You're earning consistent royalties, funding your writing dreams.
- Readers eagerly await your next release, engaging with you online and through your newsletters.

This vision is achievable if you combine dedication with the principles shared in this book. The indie author path isn't always easy, but it's a journey filled with creativity, connection, and opportunity.

Case Studies: Authors Who Took Control
1. Michael J. Sullivan
Sullivan began his career by self-publishing the *Riyria Revelations* series. Through smart marketing and a deep understanding of his audience, he transitioned to hybrid publishing while retaining control over key rights. His indie beginnings laid the foundation for a thriving career.

2. Bella Andre
Andre used the flexibility of indie publishing to dominate the romance genre. By experimenting with pricing strategies and building direct relationships with her readers, she became a bestselling author with millions of copies sold.

Your Call to Action
This book has equipped you with the tools and strategies to:
- Publish your work on your terms.
- Maximize your income and opportunities.
- Connect deeply with your audience.

Now it's time to take action:
1. Revisit your notes and prioritize the strategies that resonate most with your goals.

2. Commit to completing one major publishing or marketing milestone in the next 30 days.
3. Reflect on how far you've come, and don't be afraid to dream big for your future.

You have the power to shape your writing career on your terms. The indie author advantage is about more than royalties and control—it's about creating a life where your passion and your profession align. Embrace the freedom, stay committed to growth, and trust in your ability to achieve success.

Your journey as an indie author starts now. The possibilities are endless, and your stories are waiting to be shared with the world.

About the Author

B Alan Bourgeois began his writing journey at age 12, crafting screenplays for *Adam-12* as an outlet to develop his style. While he never submitted these works, the experience fueled his passion for storytelling. After following the conventional advice of pursuing a stable career, Bourgeois rediscovered his love for writing in 1989 through a community college class, leading to his first published short story. Since then, he has written over 48 short stories, published more than 10 books, including the award-winning *Extinguishing the Light*, and made his mark in the publishing world.

Recognizing the challenges authors face, Bourgeois founded Creative House Press in the early 2000s, publishing 60 books by other authors in five years and gaining insights into the industry's marketing needs. In 2011, he launched the Texas Authors Association, which grew to include two nonprofits promoting Texas writers and literacy. He also created innovative programs like the Lone Star Festival and short story contests for students, and in 2016, the Authors Marketing Event, offering a groundbreaking Certification program for book marketing expertise.

Despite setbacks during the COVID-19 pandemic, Bourgeois adapted by launching the Authors School of Business, providing essential tools for authors to succeed as "Authorpreneurs." As publishing evolves, he has explored NFTs as a potential revenue stream for writers. With decades of experience, Bourgeois remains a driving force in the literary community, committed to helping authors thrive in a changing industry.

Bourgeois is currently the director of the Texas Authors Museum & Institute of History, based in Austin, Texas

B Alan Bourgeois

Other Books by the Author in this Series

Y'all Write: A Month-Long Guide to Achieving Your Writing Goals

Unlock your creative potential with *Y'all Write: A Month of Writing Celebration and Growth*! This guide offers tips, motivation, and tools to help writers of all levels set goals, build momentum, and embrace the joy of storytelling.

Author's Roadmap to Success: Proven Strategies for Thriving in Publishing

Unlock the secrets to literary success with *Author's Roadmap to Success: Proven Strategies for Thriving in Publishing*. This essential guide provides actionable strategies to help writers build strong habits, master self-publishing, and thrive in their writing careers.

The Writer's Self-Care Guide: Top Ten Steps to Balance and Thrive

Transform your writing journey with *The Writer's Self-Care Guide: Top Ten Steps to Balance and Thrive*. This practical guide offers actionable steps to nurture your creativity, set boundaries, and achieve a balanced, fulfilling writing life.

Indie Author's Playbook

Top Ten Keys for Successful Writing and Productivity

Unlock your writing potential with *Top Ten Keys for Successful Writing and Productivity*. This guide offers actionable strategies to build consistent habits, manage time effectively, and produce high-quality work to elevate your writing

Mastering Research: Top Ten Steps to Research Like a Pro

Elevate your writing with *Mastering Research: Top Ten Steps to Research Like a Pro*. This essential guide provides practical tools and techniques to conduct thorough, credible research and seamlessly integrate it into your work.

Character Chronicles: Crafting Depth and Consistency in Creative Projects

Bring your characters to life with *Character Chronicles: Crafting Depth and Consistency in Creative Projects*. This essential guide reveals professional techniques to develop authentic, complex characters that resonate across any creative medium.

Editing Essentials: Your Guide to Finding the Perfect Editor

Transform your manuscript with *Editing Essentials: Your Guide to Finding the Perfect Editor*. This guide provides practical steps to identify, evaluate, and collaborate with the ideal editor to elevate your writing.

B Alan Bourgeois

AI Programs Apps Authors Should Use

Revolutionize your writing with *Top Ten AI Programs Authors Should Use*. This guide explores powerful AI tools like Grammarly and Scrivener, offering practical tips to enhance creativity, productivity, and efficiency.

The Business of Writing

Master the publishing world with *Unlocking the Business of Writing*. This essential guide provides expert advice and practical tips to build your author platform, maximize royalties, and turn your passion into a thriving career.

Creating an Effective Book Cover

Create a book cover that captivates readers with *Top Ten Keys to Creating an Effective Book Cover*. This guide offers expert tips and practical advice on design, branding, and marketing to make your book stand out.

Mastering the Art of the Sales Pitch

Master the art of the sales pitch with *Mastering the Art of the Sales Pitch*. This guide provides essential strategies to captivate your audience, highlight your book's value, and drive its success.

Indie Author's Playbook

Publishing Issues Authors Deal With

Overcome publishing challenges with *Publishing Issues Authors Deal With*. This guide offers practical strategies and expert insights to help you navigate rejection, editing, marketing, and more to achieve your publishing dreams.

The Indie Author Advantage: Mastering Control, Royalties, and Reach for Self-Publishing Success

Thrive as an indie author with *The Indie Author Advantage: Mastering Control, Royalties, and Reach for Self-Publishing Success*. This guide offers actionable strategies to retain creative control, maximize royalties, and reach a global audience.

Mastering Amazon Publishing: A Comprehensive Guide to Success for Indie Authors

Achieve self-publishing success with *Mastering Amazon Publishing: A Comprehensive Guide to Success for Indie Authors*. This guide provides proven strategies to navigate KDP, boost visibility, and maximize earnings for your books.

B Alan Bourgeois

Marketing Essentials for Authors: Proven Strategies to Boost Book Sales

Boost your book sales with *Top Ten Marketing Essentials for Authors: Proven Strategies to Promote Your Book*. This guide combines traditional and digital marketing tactics to help authors effectively connect with readers and turn their books into bestsellers.

Marketing Mastery: Avoiding Common Mistakes for Authors

Master book marketing with *Marketing Mastery: Avoiding Common Mistakes for Authors*. This guide offers actionable advice to help authors connect with readers, build a strong online presence, and achieve their publishing goals.

The Author Branding Blueprint

Elevate your writing career with *Author Brand Mastery: A Comprehensive Guide to Building and Sustaining Your Unique Identity*. This guide provides practical steps to define your brand, build a professional presence, and connect meaningfully with your audience.

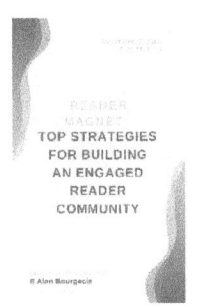

Indie Author's Playbook

Reader Magnet: Top Strategies for Building an Engaged Reader Community

Build a loyal reader community with *Reader Magnet: Top Strategies for Building an Engaged Reader Community*. This guide offers actionable strategies to connect with readers, create exclusive content, and turn your audience into passionate advocates.

Author Platform Mastery: A Comprehensive Guide to Building, Monetizing, and Growing Your Audience

Build your literary empire with *Author Platform Mastery: A Comprehensive Guide to Building, Monetizing, and Growing Your Audience*. This essential guide offers practical strategies to define your brand, engage readers, and expand your reach.

Networking Success for Authors: Essential Strategies Guide

Achieve your literary goals with *Networking Success for Authors: Essential Strategies Guide*. This practical roadmap offers strategies to build meaningful connections, promote your work, and create a supportive community for lasting success.

B Alan Bourgeois

Write, Publish, Market: The Ultimate Handbook for Author Success
ISBN:
Master the modern publishing landscape with *Write, Publish, Market: The Ultimate Handbook for Author Success*. This guide provides actionable strategies to build your author brand, attract readers, and achieve long-term success in your writing career.

Mastering Interviews: Essential Tips for Authors' Success

Excel in interviews with *Mastering Interviews: Essential Tips for Authors' Success*. This guide offers practical advice to confidently promote your work, connect with audiences, and turn every interview into a memorable success.

Mastering Event Presentations: Avoiding Common Author Mistakes

Captivate your audience with *Mastering Event Presentations: Avoiding Common Author Mistakes*. This guide offers practical strategies to avoid pitfalls, engage your audience, and deliver impactful presentations that boost your confidence and connect with readers.

Indie Author's Playbook

Survival Strategies for Indie Authors: Overcoming Challenges and Achieving Success

Thrive as an indie author with *Survival Strategies for Indie Authors: Overcoming Challenges and Achieving Success*. This guide provides practical advice and actionable tips to overcome obstacles, enhance your skills, and achieve your publishing goals.

Empowering Authors: Top Ten Strategies for Writing Success and Career Growth

Achieve your writing dreams with *Empowering Authors: Top Ten Strategies for Writing Success and Career Growth*. This guide offers practical advice and proven strategies to build habits, refine your craft, and grow your author career with confidence.

The Sacred Connection

Infuse your writing with mindfulness and purpose through *Creating with Spirit: The Sacred Art of Writing and Publishing*. This guide transforms your creative journey into a spiritual practice, empowering you to inspire readers and overcome challenges with authenticity and intention.

B Alan Bourgeois

Beyond the Basics: Advanced Strategies for Indie Author Success
ISBN:
Elevate your indie publishing career with *Beyond the Basics: Advanced Strategies for Indie Author Success*. This guide offers actionable tips and strategies to diversify income, engage readers, and build a sustainable, thriving career.

The AI Author: Embracing the Future of Fiction

Embrace the future of storytelling with *The AI Author: Balancing Efficiency and Creativity in Fiction Writing*. This guide helps authors harness AI to boost productivity and creativity while preserving the emotional depth and artistry of creating.

The Non-Fiction Nexus: Balancing AI and Human Insight in the Future of Writing

Elevate your non-fiction writing with *The Non-Fiction Nexus: Balancing AI and Human Insight in the Future of Writing*. This guide shows how to harness AI's efficiency while preserving the creativity and ethical judgment that make your work truly impactful.

Indie Author's Playbook

Authorship Reimagined: NFTs and Blockchain Essentials
ISBN:
Embrace the future of publishing with *NFT and Blockchain Essentials for Authors' Success*. This guide explains how blockchain and NFTs can protect your work, automate royalties, and expand your audience while maximizing revenue.

Adapting Success: Your Book's Journey to Film

Turn your book into a cinematic sensation with *From Page to Screen: A Step-by-Step Guide to Adapting Your Book into a Blockbuster Film*. This guide provides practical advice and industry insights to help you navigate the adaptation process and bring your story to life on the big screen.

Beyond the Basics: Advanced Strategies for Indie Author Success
Elevate your indie publishing career with this ultimate guide to mastering advanced strategies in writing, marketing, and global distribution. Packed with actionable tips and real-world examples, it empowers authors to balance creativity with entrepreneurship and build sustainable, thriving careers.

B Alan Bourgeois

2026: The Ultimate Year for Indie Authors

Make 2026 your breakthrough year with *The Ultimate Year for Indie Authors*. This guide offers practical strategies to optimize publishing, leverage social media, and achieve unparalleled success in your indie author journey.